Basic Christian Beliefs

Basic Christian Beliefs

W. BURNET EASTON, JR.

Philadelphia
THE WESTMINSTER PRESS

Library of Congress Catalog Card No.: 57–8930

PRINTED IN THE UNITED STATES OF AMERICA

To
E. W. E.
Philippians 1:3-5

Contents

Preface 9
I. Two Approaches 13
II. The Authority of the Bible 34
III. God 46
IV. Man 75
V. Jesus, Who Is the Christ 97
VI. The Significance of Jesus Who Is the Christ 117
VII. The Church 136
VIII. The Kingdom of God 158
Notes 188
Index 193

Preface

AS ALMOST EVERYONE IS AWARE, WE IN AMERICA TODAY APPEAR TO be in the midst of a religious revival. Church attendance has reached an all-time high, and is still going up; since World War II it has grown faster than the population. Almost every " slick paper " magazine carries religious articles. Billboards, radio, and TV advise us to go to church on Sunday. In some parts of the country even major football games are begun with public prayer. These and many other illustrations are well known to almost everyone, and, as never before in the last couple of hundred years, there is widespread general agreement that " religion is a good thing."

Probably we who are Christians should be grateful for this renewed interest in religion. At least it opens doors of opportunity where they were closed before. Nevertheless, " all is not gold that glitters," and there are some very grave dangers in this religious revival from a Christian point of view. Much of the return to religion is not a return to Christianity with a cutting edge; rather, it is a return to a " vague religiosity " and to " spiritual values " undefined. We should not forget that, according to the Bible, religion is *not* necessarily " a good thing." It can be idolatrous and it can become a kind of opiate or substitute for a genuine Christian faith. The Bible condemns nothing more vigorously than false religions. A religious revival that is just a return to " religion in general " will evaporate about as fast as it developed. Just as a person cannot learn language in general but must learn some particular language, so must a person who wants a meaningful religion come to some real understanding of a particular religion.

What is not understood by a vast number of people today is that Christianity is a particular and a precise religion. It involves far more than a belief in some kind of supreme being, called God, plus approval of a morality more or less based on the ethics of Jesus. To become a Christian is to become something rather precise; and the preciseness of the Christian faith, which sets it off from other religions, can be stated for the purposes of clarification and communication in a set of reasonable and understandable doctrines or beliefs. And these doctrines are not just abstract philosophical propositions of interest only to theologians. They can be understood by anyone with a little effort (although they may not be accepted by everyone), for they have been hammered out in the experience of daily living. The Christian doctrines can be as exciting as life itself, and we who are Christians believe that, properly understood, they make more sense out of life than anything else does. The tragedy is that multitudes of people who are returning to religion do not know what the basic Christian beliefs are, nor the very sound reasons for them.

This book is an attempt to explain the Christian religion in rather simple, and I hope readable, language for the beginner who wants to know what Christianity stands for, how it fits together, what the reasons for it are, and how it is related to the practical business of living. By the term "beginner" I have in mind three different groups: first, students in courses in colleges and in Church foundation centers on university campuses, and also in introductory courses in seminaries; secondly, lay people who would like to know more clearly about the formulation and defense of the faith they profess; thirdly, those who are now outside the faith but who are curious and searching and who would like to know, in brief compass, what Christianity is all about before getting themselves involved.

With this purpose in mind, it is obvious that this presentation will be somewhat simplified. I have merely tried to put together and interpret in a readable fashion what seems to me the best thinking that is going on among Christian thinkers today. Needless to say, I am indebted to many people — teachers, writers, my students — far more than I can recall or acknowledge. However, the material in Chapter II has been rewritten from two articles that appeared originally in *Motive* magazine (November and December, 1953), on "Is the Bible Alive Today?" and "How to Read the Bible." I wish to thank the editors of *Motive* for the kind permission to re-use that material. The quotation from Pierre Maury at the end of Chapter VI was copied from some magazine I have since unfortunately lost. I wish to thank the Division of Christian Education of the National Council of the Churches of Christ in the U.S.A. for permission to use quotations from the Revised Standard Version of the Bible, which version is used unless otherwise noted. Lastly, I owe a special debt of gratitude to Miss Katherine McConnell for her cheerful help in typing the manuscript.

W. B. E. Jr.

Park College
Parkville, Missouri

CHAPTER

I

Two Approaches

SOMEWHERE, I DO NOT NOW RECALL WHERE, I READ A STORY OF A MAN who, in the last century, got on a tram car and could not find a seat. He announced in a loud voice, "I am an atheist!" Immediately so many horrified people got off that he had a choice of any number of seats. That was seventy-five or more years ago. Today, in such a situation, a few people might feel uncomfortable, but it is doubtful that any would give up their seats in a bus just because a confessed atheist entered. The few, if any, who did leave would be looked upon as the odd ones. This shift in the average reaction to the atheist says a great deal about the presentation of religion, especially a positive Christian faith, in the mid-twentieth century. Recently one of my students in a course on the Christian religion asked why I presented Christianity so apologetically. "Why do you spend so much time defending and explaining?" he asked. "Why don't you just lay it on the line?" I gave him a book to read which presents the faith forcefully and without apology. A week later he was back and said: "This book makes me mad! It tells you what to believe, but not why! The author does not justify his position!" Even the people who say they want the Christian truth want to have it adequately and intelligently defended. Most people today are not going to believe something unless it makes sense in terms that they think makes sense, and many have grave doubts about how much sense Christianity makes. In a religious way this is the greatest revolution of our time.

The simple fact is that we have had not only political, social, economic, and industrial revolutions, but also an intellectual revolution which affects what men believe about how truth is determined. And this is the most significant revolution of all. The world-view in which Christianity was born, grew up, and reached its maturity has gone. We of the twentieth century live in a totally different culture. In the first century, and indeed through the Middle Ages, men generally believed that the world was flat and that it was the center of the universe. Heaven was up in the sky and hell under the earth. If two or three normally reliable people said they saw an extraordinary occurrence, which they reported as a miracle, such an explanation satisfied men's minds. They had no curiosity about cause and effect, or what today we call scientific proof. This situation no longer obtains. Since Copernicus, our neat, self-contained world has become a mere mote in seemingly devastating space. More important, the results of rigidly applied rational empirical methods, i.e., those of science and of reason based on demonstrable facts of experience, have revealed that many things we thought were true, even things claimed as true by the Christian Church, simply are not true.

In our time, for most people truth has pretty largely become what can be proved true before the bar of reason on empirically established evidence. But the Christian faith rests on truth established by faith and revelation. In earlier days the validity of revelation as a legitimate method of discovering truth was accepted completely. Even Descartes, who lived in the seventeenth century and who is the "father" of the modern scientific method, made a place in his system for the truth of revealed truth. Today, however, even those who accept the truth of revelation have their backs to the wall. To themselves as well as to others they have to justify this claim, and it is not easy. It is not easy because of the revolution in the world-view of the average educated person.

Thus, the defenders of Biblical Christianity find themselves in a new situation today. They must defend a faith that grew up in one culture, with the inevitable language forms and thought patterns from that culture, in terms of a vastly different culture with different thought patterns. Therefore, if Biblical Christianity is to become a power in the lives of men and women today, it must of necessity be "apologetic," that is, it must seek to make itself clear and compelling in terms modern man can understand and accept. To do this is difficult. It is not surprising that the faithful, in attempting to defend the faith against the changed world-view, have frequently fallen into one of two errors. On the one hand the orthodox or fundamentalists, in order to protect what they believe to be the essentials of the faith, have retreated into an authoritarian, doctrinaire dogmatism which seems to those who cannot accept such a position to compel intellectual and moral hara-kiri. On the other hand, much of the so-called liberal Christianity seems to have committed the greater crime of being willing to abandon any of the essentials of the faith every time they did not fit the latest scientific fad. The question is: How to avoid the Scylla of intellectual obscurantism and the Charybdis of such watered-down faith that it can no longer be properly called the Christian faith? To put the question another way: How is one to make clear a faith that grew up in one world-view for persons who have a different world-view, without sacrificing either intelligence or the essential givens of the faith?

This book is one attempt to answer these questions.

1. The Issues Defined

If what has been said above about the shift in world-view is true, and if men today are seeking for answers in empirical rational terms before they will believe anything, then there is raised the question of the relation of faith to reason as methods of discovering the truth. There is a lot of confusion at this point, which arises from the rather widespread opinion that faith and reason are completely opposed: if you live by one, you must deny the other. This conflict is not so real as is often imagined.

Before going on, however, and by way of clarification, it should be pointed out that part of the confusion arises from the fact that the word "faith" is used in two somewhat different ways. First, faith frequently, perhaps usually for most people, means the intellectual acceptance of certain propositions or ideas as being true that are not susceptible to normal methods of rational empirical proof. Secondly, faith means to act and to make decisions in terms of these propositions — even when there may be some intellectual doubt about their validity. It is only with the second definition that Christianity is concerned, for Christianity is not interested in establishing merely a set of theoretical propositions; it is primarily interested in the actual business of living — acting and making decisions. Unfortunately, however, this has not always been understood. Having faith has frequently been defined as intellectual acceptance of certain theoretical propositions, or, as the schoolboy once defined it, "Faith is believing what you know ain't so!" Most unfortunate of all, it is quite possible to give intellectual assent to certain beliefs but not actually to live in terms of them. Thus, perhaps the greatest weakness of our churches is the number of members who willingly recite the creeds, who say they believe in God, and in Christ, who are honestly shocked to hear these beliefs doubted or denied, but who do not actually make their daily decisions as though there were a God who has revealed himself in Christ. This is a travesty on the word "faith" in any Christian sense. Faith becomes real only when it becomes a basis for decision and action. In this sense, the man who intellectually may have some doubt about Christ but tries to live in terms of him is more Christian than the man who professes to believe in Christ with absolute certainty but who orders his life by something other than that revelation.

Sören Kierkegaard's famous illustration from Socrates is the best I know. Kierkegaard points out that intellectually Socrates admitted that he was uncertain whether or not there was life after death. Socrates' argument in *The Apology* seems to indicate that he believed the probability lay on the side of immortality, but he was by no means certain of it. In spite of this intellectual doubt, however, Socrates was willing to make his faith decisive and accept death for his convictions. Kierkegaard writes of him:

"Let us consider Socrates. Nowadays everyone dabbles in a few proofs; some have several such proofs, others fewer. But Socrates! He puts the question objectively in a problematic manner: if there is an immortality. On this 'if' he risks his entire life; he has the courage to meet death. . . . Can any better proof be given for the immortality of the soul? But those who have the three proofs do not at all determine their lives in conformity therewith; if there is an immortality, it must feel disgust over their manner of life." [1]

Christians are not interested in an abstract intellectual faith, but only in what is called existential faith, the faith that is completely involved in the decisions and resulting actions of human existence.

With this understanding of the meaning of faith, we are ready to consider its relation to reason. In a general and perhaps oversimplified way, it is fair to say that those who think about this problem, the philosophers and theologians, fall into two major schools of thought: the naturalists, who insist that all reality is limited to the natural world; and the supranaturalists, who insist that there is a supranatural reality, in some sense, external to the natural world. Within both schools there are many varieties and subdivisions, and there are some who try to bridge the gap, such as those who start with naturalism and try to show that it leads to a supranaturalism. Then there are those who would say that the idealists, who hold that the ultimate nature of reality is ideal or spirit, have a third position. All idealists, however, eventually fall into either the naturalist or the supranaturalist camp, depending on whether they conceive of the ideal, or spirit, as being a part of the natural world, or as independent and external to it. In spite of this confusion, the two categories of natural and supranatural are useful, and every man ultimately is forced to start with one of the two conflicting assumptions.

In general, the naturalists, of whatever variety, insist that all true knowledge that we can have must be based upon and limited to what can be discovered in the natural world and deduced from it by logical proof and empirically demonstrated reason. Since the supranatural cannot be empirically proved to exist, it is illegitimate to talk about it or use it as a basis of knowledge. In making such a statement, however, it should immediately be added that for many modern philosophical naturalists the meaning and content of " nature " includes far more than the average man on the street realizes. The older, narrower naturalism, which limited itself pretty largely to materialism, matter-in-motion, and chemistry, has been seriously challenged, even by men who call themselves naturalists. For these naturalists, man is a part of and must be completely understood as a product of the natural world. However, they recognize that man is a being who thinks, reasons, has aspirations and emotions, and develops systems of values to which he gives loyalties. All of this can be empirically demonstrated; therefore, these " spiritual " aspects of man must be included in the term " naturalism."

Much of the debate among naturalists revolves around just how these spiritual aspects of man should be interpreted and what they imply. Again, to oversimplify somewhat, the naturalists fall into two major schools. First are those who can be called the atheistic naturalists. These say that man's spiritual qualities are simply the product of nature and natural processes and that they have been produced by a mysterious chain of historical accidents. This is all there is. No external power is needed to explain man's situation and man is ultimately alone in the universe. This situation is admittedly pathetic, but it is honest and realistic; man can achieve a certain kind of dignity in accepting the situation. " We must build on the firm foundation of unyielding despair " (Russell). Granted this tragic situation, each man must make his decision in terms of what seems best to him and achieve satisfaction in assuming responsibility for making these decisions (Sartre). But there is nothing ultimate. God is only an illusion, and belief in him is simply an escape device of people who are afraid to face the facts (Freud).

Then there are what are called the theistic naturalists. These philosophers also try to explain man's situation completely in terms of natural phenomena, but they claim that when we examine the totality of nature and the development of man, including his spiritual nature, we discover that *within, not outside,* the world there is a process going on that makes for values, and that men live more richly if and when they live in terms of this process. The process, for want of a better term, they say, can be called God, if it is thoroughly understood that the term "God" is completely limited to the process and not in any sense transcendent or outside. Writes Henry N. Wieman, one of the leading American exponents of this position, who calls himself an empirical theist:

> "Even theology has sought to portray God as a reality beyond time and space. . . . God so understood can have no intrinsic value. . . . God must be found in actual events. . . . The ultimate cause of this creation of meaning in human life is nothing else than the total order of happenings necessary for it to take place. To seek a cause beyond events is, in the view here defended, a self-defeating and self-contradictory endeavor." [2]

Thus the naturalists differ among themselves as to the ultimate interpretation of their data, and even what data can be legitimately included, but they unite in insisting that all we can know must come from the natural world and the conclusions drawn from it by the rational, empirical method. They unite in accusing the supranaturalists of being irrational because the supranaturalists claim that the world, including man and his spiritual aspects, cannot be understood in terms of simple naturalism but that some supranatural being (God) is necessary. They accuse the supranaturalists of positing an irrational faith which cannot be proved by any human tests.

Certainly at first glance the argument seems to be all on the side of the naturalists. No one has seen God. Supranaturalists cannot prove, in naturalists' terms, that God is. Whether we sweep the skies with our most powerful telescopes or delve into the structure of the atom with the most powerful instruments, no one has ever found anything that could be remotely identified as God, or even a place where God might be said to reside. Since Biblical faith rests on a supranatural basis, it has to justify its claims, and it has to justify them in terms that make at least as much sense to modern man as the claims of the naturalists. To this task we now turn.

2. Faith and Reason

First of all, however, at the risk of being redundant, but in order that there may be no misunderstanding or equivocation, it must be re-emphasized that Biblical Christianity is a supranaturalistic religion. It is based upon the conviction that there is a supranatural God and a supranatural world. One may or may not accept this faith, but if one does not, he ought to be honest enough not to call himself a Christian, even though he is a very fine person and gives allegiance to some or all of the ethical principles of Christianity. Further, it must be made clear that these claims of Christianity (and hereafter, unless specifically stated to the contrary, I mean Biblical Christianity by the term " Christianity ") rest upon faith and faith alone. Christianity accepts as valid the truth of revelation from a God who is in some sense transcendent and outside of the natural world, but both the validity of that revelation and the actuality of God are acts of faith. As our Lord demonstrated in his earthly work, as the apostles affirmed and taught, and as the Reformation rediscovered, " we are justified by faith." Any attempt to water down or modify this position is to change Christianity into something it is not.

Such a statement seems to sharpen the conflict between faith and reason. Properly understood, however, this conflict is not so acute as it at first appears. To live by faith is not so irrational as its opponents claim, and to live by pure reason is a human impossibility. Actually, to state the issue as faith versus reason is to state a false antithesis.

Supranaturalists are not necessarily antirationalists. They too find a very important place for reason; they too recognize that in a very real sense even their supranatural faith must answer at the bar of reason. When all is said and done, we are men and only men, that is, we are creatures bound to this world by the conditions of our creatureliness. (Whether or not man also in some sense transcends the conditions of his creatureliness is a question to be considered later.) One of the conditions of this creatureliness is that all that we know, we know, in one way or another, only through our minds and our reason. We may fail pretty badly in the attempt because our thinking may be defective, but all men try to make sense out of their world and their lives. If the supranaturalist insists upon a supranaturalistic faith, it is because, in the last analysis, he is convinced that supranaturalism makes the most sense — is the most reasonable — when the totality of the human situation is taken into consideration. Even Tertullian, who made the most extreme statement in this regard — "I believe because it is absurd" — made it because it appealed to him as being the most reasonable understanding of the human situation. If it had not made sense to him, he could not have made it. The supranaturalists in their assertion of the necessity for supranaturalism also submit to the bar of reason. In this regard they are not different from the naturalists in method.

Neither is the reason of the naturalists as pure and devoid of faith as they would sometimes have us believe. When we face realistically the mysteries of the universe and of human existence and ask the ultimate questions, "Why?" and "What?," there are no absolutely certain and provable answers. When we seriously ask the questions: "Why is there a world at all?" "Why is there not nothing?" "What is the meaning of human existence?" "Why are there beings on this earth who ask these questions?," etc., there are no final answers that are not answers based on unprovable assumptions, on faith. All any man can do, regardless of what persuasion of thought or philosophy he holds, is to look at his world with all its mystery and complexity and say, "I believe it is this, or that"; but to say it is absolutely "this" or "that" is not only arrogance, it is also dishonest thinking. The naturalist is caught in this dilemma as much as the supranaturalist, and the naturalist's position is as much based on unprobable assumptions, on faith, as the supranaturalist's position. As Alan Richardson has put it:

"Faith is not a short cut; it is not a substitute for understanding but a condition of it. . . . Between faith and reason there can be no conflict, for faith is ancillary to reason; faith cannot oppose reason: it can oppose only other faiths, which are being used as rival conditions or presuppositions of reason. . . . The fact that Christian faith is opposed to rationalism . . . should not lead us to suppose that it is itself opposed to reason, for rationalism operates only through the employment of a concealed faith-principle which is nonetheless as necessary to it as is faith to Christian philosophy." [3]

The simple fact is that such knowledge as we have is possible only because of prior assumptions which are neither more nor less than assumptions of faith. In other words, there is no knowledge that does not arise out of "the faith situation." Christians have long asserted that before one can have confidence in God he must first have some belief in God, or at least a willingness to consider the possibility favorably, and that religious truth comes only from a prior religious faith. Opponents of Christianity have often accused Christians of wish-thinking in this regard. They point out that if one wishes to believe something badly enough, he can make himself believe it and may even get help from it; but the belief is not necessarily true, it may be merely imagination. There is certainly a great deal of truth in this accusation. The human mind seems to be such that it can frequently make itself believe what it wants. Sometimes it makes itself believe some pretty weird things. Unfortunately, none have been more weird than some of the ideas some Christians have made themselves believe. Yes, this accusation has some truth in it, but—and this is what these critics of the religious approach forget—the accusation is a two-edged sword! It applies not only to Christians, it applies to all knowledge and all people, including those making the criticism. There is no knowledge in any area without prior assumptions of faith, without at least a willingness to consider a proposition favorably. For instance, if you say that you wish to discover whatever truth there is revealed in physics, or in psychology, but at the same time refuse to believe in either the basic assumptions or methods of these subjects, you will not get very far. At best you will learn some interesting facts other people oddly believe but which are irrelevant as far as you are concerned. In order to discover truth in anything, it is first necessary to have some faith. No one escapes this situation. The frequent tragedy is that one group, making one set of assumptions, claims that its assumptions are not assumptions but proof, while their opponents are operating on naïve faith.

Arthur Koestler in his novel *Arrival and Departure* has a profound illustration of this human dilemma. Toward the end of the story his hero, who is about to return to the underground movement, writes his girl, who has escaped to America expecting him to follow her, as follows:

"Today I am going to fly off at a tangent from the twisted path. I have not many illusions about why I am doing it, nor about the cause which I serve. As children we used to be given a curious kind of puzzle to play with. It was a paper with a tangle of very thin blue and red lines. If you just looked at it, you couldn't make out anything. But if you covered it with a piece of transparent red tissue paper, the red lines of the drawing disappeared and the blue lines formed a picture —a clown holding a circus hoop and a little dog jumping through. And if you covered the same drawing with blue tissue paper, a roaring lion appeared, chasing the clown across the ring. You can do the same with every mortal living or dead. You can look at them through Sonia's tissue paper and write a biography of Napoleon in terms of his pituitary gland. . . . You can explain the message of the prophets as epileptical foam and the Sistine Madonna as the projection of an incestuous dream. The method is correct and the picture itself complete. But beware of the arrogant error of believing it is the only one. The picture you see through the blue tissue paper will be no less true and complete."[4]

Looked at realistically and honestly, life is a "paper with a tangle of very thin blue and red lines" (and many others as well). In order to make any sense out of it at all, it is our human dilemma that we must impose certain "tissue papers," certain assumptions of faith. This is inescapable, and in itself should warn us that there are limits to human reasoning. Moreover, this illustration reveals a further very important fact about human life and human understanding, namely, that the tissue paper, the assumptions we start with, have already largely determined the final conclusion that we will reach. If a man assumes that all the data he can legitimately accept are limited to natural phenomena and natural processes, and that all transcendent or supranatural data must be rigorously denied, it is inevitable that he will reach naturalistic conclusions. If, on the other hand, he assumes that there are, or that there may be, some supranatural data which are legitimate, he will come to a different conclusion. *If our thinking is consistent, the conclusions we arrive at have already been determined by our original presuppositions and basic assumptions.* This is a further limitation on the possibilities of human reason and should illustrate what is meant by saying there is no truth or knowledge outside of " the faith situation."

The importance of this cannot be overestimated in any discussion of religion, or of anything else of importance, for that matter. Unfortunately, many very able and brilliant people fail to recognize either that it is impossible to think at all without assumptions or that the assumptions are the most important factors in determining the final answer, or both. Recently I attended a philosophical meeting where a brilliant professor defended the thesis that any metaphysics at all was impossible because every metaphysics starts with some unprovable assumptions. As long as his critics accepted his empirical, rational assumptions, which most of them did, he defended himself ably and well. When, however, it was pointed out to him that his whole position also rested on unprovable assumptions, namely, that all truth must be limited to empirically verifiable data, and that he was guilty of the very thing of which he accused the metaphysicians, he was completely nonplused. Finally and rather reluctantly he admitted, " I never thought of that."

To summarize the argument so far in this section: Although there are many variations within each group, all men are ultimately either naturalists or supranaturalists, and the conclusions they reach about the world, religion, and the meaning of life, if they are consistent thinkers, are inevitably quite different. The issue, however, of faith versus reason in the terms in which the conflict usually rages is not clear-cut. Actually, both naturalists and supranaturalists employ both faith and reason. Both groups make assumptions as to what data they will accept, which, strictly speaking, can only be called assumptions of faith. Both groups make the assumptions they do because making those particular assumptions seems to them most reasonable. If such an analysis is correct, it at least leaves the door as wide open for an intelligent supranaturalism, and thus for Biblical Christianity, as it does for naturalism.

3. Which Faith?

The issue, then, is not between faith and no faith, nor is it between faith and reason; rather, it is between different faiths. One of the common false distinctions which creates a lot of confusion is the distinction that says that Christian or religious people are people of faith while atheists and skeptics are people without faith. Nothing could be farther from the truth, for it is impossible for a person to live without any faith. As was noted above, before the mystery of the universe and the question, "Why is there a world?" all any man can do is look at his world and say, "I believe." The atheist is just as much a man of faith as the theist; he simply operates on a different set of unprovable assumptions. Because of this inescapable human situation, the question of the relation of faith to reason is not solved by simply abandoning religious faith. That is like jumping from the frying pan into the fire. Therefore, the ultimate question about which all men must decide and about which they actually do decide, unconsciously if not consciously, is the question, "What faith shall I live by?" Since this is so, and since all men, in trying to answer the ultimate questions of life, fall into one of the two major schools of thought, naturalism or supranaturalism, it may be well to consider briefly these two approaches to the question of religion. Let us first consider the naturalists.

The position of the naturalists might be characterized like this: They look at the world and try to conclude what the meaning is. Because they insist that all conclusions must be limited to natural facts taken from the world and that any outside or supranatural reference is illegitimate, they have no perspective beyond the world and are caught in their own multitudinous data. Consequently they end in an anarchy of interpretations, no one of them more valid than another.

To make a simple analogy: One man, A, looks at the world and its data and concludes that there probably is a God and that he is a Circle. But B comes along and says: "No, you have not interpreted the data quite correctly. If you will look at the data more clearly, you will see it is not a Circle; it is a Square." Then C enters the discussion: "Neither of you fellows is quite right. There is some data you have not considered seriously enough. It is neither a Circle nor a Square; it's a Triangle." At this point D, an agnostic or skeptic, says: "You fellows may be partly right; perhaps there is something there. But you obviously can't agree among yourselves. As I read the data, nobody can say what it is. It's just a big Question Mark." Finally along comes E, an atheist, who says: "All of you are kidding yourselves. You merely want to believe in something because you are afraid not to. There is nothing there except the projection of your own thinking." And the significant fact in all this is that no one can prove that any one of the others is wrong. Naturalism has in fact ended in an anarchy of opinions, no one of which can honestly establish itself as absolute or can give ultimate meaning to life. This is why our time, which marks the fruition of naturalism, has produced relativism as its most dominant expression, a relativism that cuts the nerve of meaning and action and disturbs even some of the more discerning naturalists.

The charge is frequently made that the supranaturalists also present an anarchy of opinions. There is some truth in this charge if supranaturalism is broadly interpreted, as the study of comparative religion reveals. Nevertheless, all high religions unite in pointing, one way or another, to one Supreme Being. Within the context of Christianity, which is the form of supranaturalism we are primarily concerned to defend, there is remarkable agreement, far more than a superficial reference to the many Christian sects would indicate. Orthodox Christianity, whether Protestant,

Roman Catholic, Greek Orthodox, or what not, agrees in affirming the reality of a transcendent and supranatural God who is the author of life and the guarantor of good, and who incarnated himself in Jesus of Nazareth who is the Christ, for our help and salvation. On these and other central Christian doctrines — resurrection, judgment, atonement, forgiveness — there is no disagreement. Such disagreements as exist among Christians are in the realm of how these central affirmatives are to be applied. These differences are admittedly serious and tragic, especially when they are given undue importance, as seems so often to be the case. But it should be emphasized that on the central faith and on the answers to the ultimate questions Christians do present a united front to the world. (It is also true that some people, in our time a great many, have developed non-Biblical philosophies and kept the label "Christian." This has added to the confusion, but Christians cannot be blamed for it.)

The reason for this degree of unity found among Christians especially, and also among other supranaturalists, is that their approach to the ultimate questions is a totally different one from that of the naturalists. Instead of taking the world and man's life in it as the primary facts of data from which all thinking must start, by which all thinking must be limited, and all conclusions drawn, as do the naturalists, the supranaturalists insist that the primary fact of data from which all thinking and conclusions must be derived is God — a God who, in some sense, is external to the world and transcends it; a God who created this world and all that is in it. This is the primary assumption of the supranaturalists and, as we have seen, it is at least as legitimate an assumption as that of the naturalist, but it produces very different conclusions. As far as it affects the religious question, it means that the history of religions is seen not primarily as the product of men's wishful thinking and not as the illusions men have created to solve their unsolved problems. Rather, the history of religions is seen as a history of God's activity and concern for men, of God revealing himself to men as rapidly as men were able to receive it.

The question may be raised: Why did God take so long to reveal himself to men, particularly if men needed that revelation? Why did he wait until the first century of the Christian Era to make his ultimate revelation in Jesus Christ? In one sense there is no answer to this question. We are men, not God. But it seems axiomatic that if there be a God, he can reveal himself to men *only* in terms men can understand within the context of the particular stage of thinking and culture they are in at the time. If God were to reveal himself to people in one cultural context in terms of a totally different culture, the revelation would be meaningless and consequently not a revelation. Therefore, it is not surprising that the earlier forms of religion, particularly in their ethical and metaphysical expressions, seem very crude to a later age. But these crudities can also be seen as preparation for a new development. The amazing fact, at least in Biblical religion, is not that of the crudities reported in the Bible, but that Biblical man was able to receive revelations somewhat in advance of his surrounding culture. When all men worshiped God in the form of idols and graven images, the Hebrews were able to understand that the God who is God is too mysterious, high, and holy to be captured in any graven image, and that all idols are something less than God. When other peoples thought of God as capricious, the Hebrews discovered that he is consistently righteous. When other peoples, even most of the Hebrews, thought in terms of many gods, some, like the great prophets, understood that God is one, and that he is the Lord of history before whom the nations of the world "are accounted as the dust on the scales" (Isa. 40:15). And then, "when the time had fully come," that is, after sufficient preparation and when at least some men were ready to receive it and spread it, "God sent forth his Son" (Gal. 4:4).

The truly amazing characteristic of the development of Biblical religion is not its crudities, not that some of the beliefs about God now seem to us barbaric and even unethical; that is merely normal expectancy. The amazing thing in the Bible is the way God was preparing man to receive ever more significant revelations of himself, and the way, time and again, men were able to receive new understanding when there was no sociological reason why they should. Thus the history of religions is seen not as the crazy attempt of man creating illusions to solve his problems; the history of religions is seen as preparation for the reception, " when the time had fully come," of God's ultimate revelation in a man, Jesus of Nazareth, who was also the Christ. (And it had to be a man because men, being men, can understand best the life of a man. This is also normal expectancy.) And since Christianity and Christianity alone (as we shall see later) answers the fundamental questions of the meaning of existence, all religions anywhere that raise and try to answer these questions — and this is what all religions do — in one way or another serve a preparation for Christianity.

This conclusion is, of course, worlds apart from that of the naturalists. But if there be a supranatural God, as the supranaturalists assume, who is the primary fact of all data and the beginning point for all thinking, then the conclusions are logical and reasonable — just as logical and just as reasonable as the conclusions of the naturalists from their assumptions. And now, having, I hope, sharpened and made clear the distinction between the position of the naturalists and that of the supranaturalists, I come to the question: Which is right? Which is true? That is *the question*. It is probably the most important question anyone has to decide.

4. The Christian Answer

As we have seen above, both these assumptions are only assumptions and are unprovable, at least on any basis of empirical proof. Therefore, both are positions of faith. But as we have also seen, all intelligent men do what they do and believe what they believe because it appears reasonable and good, at least in their opinion. The question then arises, Is there any way we can decide which of these assumptions is true?

First of all, in trying to answer this crucial question we must recognize that for finite men with limited capacities the truth must always be the truth as understood by men, and the only way in which we can arrive at what we call truth is by the long-tested standards that thoughtful men have established. In some sense we all seek pragmatic, practical working results. Even in the strictly materialistic scientific realm our truths are, strictly speaking, only practical working truths. For instance, we say that it is true that two parts of hydrogen and one part of oxygen make up water. What we mean is that this combination always has made up water and, assuming that the laws of the material world will continue to hold as constantly as they have so far, it will continue to result in water. For the ordinary practical affairs of life, such a truth is very useful, in fact necessary, and most of us are willing to say, "It is true enough to call true." But this is still different from saying that it is absolute truth. Perhaps tomorrow something will happen, or some scientist will discover conditions under which two parts of hydrogen and one part oxygen will not make water. For many years Newtonian physics was believed to be the truth and many great and practical discoveries were made on the basis of Newton's laws. Today Einstein's physics has largely displaced Newtonian physics. Even in the physical world absolute truth is more elusive than many people realize. In the spiritual realm, the realm of meanings and values, the establishment of absolute truth is even more difficult and more subjective. A value or a meaning becomes truth for us only when we put faith in it and act upon it (although we may first apply tests). This is another way of saying that truth is discovered only in "the faith situation."

Nevertheless, we all have some sense of truth, and in general what we mean by truth is that which works, that which answers the problem. Within our human limitations and in the scientific sense a proposition is said to be true when it offers a workable answer to all the questions and all the problems raised. An honest scientist does not say he has the true solution to a problem until he has demonstrated many times that it solves all the questions involved. The scientific method starts with what looks like a good hypothesis, tests it by raising all the questions possible, and sees if the hypothesis answers those questions. If it does, the hypothesis can be called true; if it does not, then it is not true. This scientific approach offers a method for testing the truth of our two assumptions.

Supranaturalism, at least Christian supranaturalism, claims that it answers the basic questions of the fundamental meaning of existence which naturalism answers either very inadequately or not at all. Biblical religion has answers to the questions of the ultimate "Why?" and the ultimate "What?" In the rest of this book we shall consider these answers in more detail, but for the moment: In its faith in a transcendent God who is the Creator, it has an answer to the questions, "Why is there a world?" and "Why is there not nothing?" In its faith in the redemption revealed in Jesus Christ, it has an answer to the meaning of existence. In its faith in the resurrection and the Kingdom of God, it has an answer to the question of destiny and a solution to the problem of evil. Biblical Christian faith has answers to these questions and its answers are not just theoretical abstractions. They are made concrete in a historical person, in Jesus who is the Christ, and they have been tested in the experience of "ten thousand times ten thousand" down through the ages.

The naturalists may not like the Christian answers, and, indeed, on the basis of their presuppositions they must reject them in whole or in part; but they cannot deny that they are answers. Some of the naturalists, particularly the various philosophical theists, are so attracted to the Christian assumptions that they try to arrive at them by other methods, but without much success. The god of the philosophers is something far less than the God who incarnated himself in Jesus Christ, and the naturalistic philosophers have great trouble with the resurrection, which is central to Christianity. Either they deny it or they reduce it to something far different from the New Testament meaning. Others in the naturalistic schools who are more realistic admit that they fail to find the answers to the ultimate questions. They try to solve their dilemma by a most amazing procedure and one that seems to me, at least, highly irrational, especially for people who claim to be scientific rationalists. Since their naturalistic systems admittedly cannot answer the ultimate questions, they claim that these questions are irrelevant and they deny the right of the supranaturalists to raise them. Thus Julian Huxley states:

> "A scientifically based philosophy enables us in the first place to cease from tormenting ourselves with questions that ought not to be asked because they cannot be answered — such as questions about First Cause, or Creation, or Ultimate Reality." [5]

Apparently Mr. Huxley's naturalistic system is pretty complete and airtight; it answers all the questions — provided you ask only the right ones! But you must not ask questions the system admittedly cannot answer!

Could anything be more unscientific, more irrational, than to insist that, just because a given system is attractive in some of its aspects and answers some questions, raising questions that it cannot answer is illegitimate? The simple fact, as empirically demonstrable as anything can be, is that men do raise these ultimate questions. That is part of the given data which must be considered. And if the nature of the universe is such that it produces beings who raise "unanswerable" questions about the meaning of their existence, then it is too diabolical to endure. Any system of thought that has a right to claim that it is the truth has to answer all the questons implied in human existence and not merely the easy ones. Christianity is such a system; it is honest and it is realistic. It recognizes that the questions implied in existence are real questions which must be answered — and it answers them. If the Christian answers are logically worked out and thoroughly tested in human experience, then they have a right to claim to be the truth in so far as it is humanly possible to speak of the truth.

I have tried to show in this chapter that a supranatural and therefore a Christian approach to the question of truth and of knowledge (what is technically called the epistemological question) is as sound and as "rational" as the naturalistic approach. Further, I have tried to show that a Christian supranaturalism answers the basic questions of life better than naturalism, although much of the elaboration and defense of these answers remains to be given. In what I have so far written, I have had to speak of Christianity as a "system." One concluding word of warning is necessary. Strictly speaking, Christianity is not a system at all. To speak of it as such is a concession to the limitations of language for the sake of a point. The Bible is not a treatise in systematic theology. The Bible and Biblical Christianity are concerned with revealing and mediating to men a way of life by which they can become new, free men—be "reborn," as John calls it, become "new creations," as Paul calls it. The "rebirth" is not a system; it is a living experience. Yet when we Christians try to explain this experience intelligibly to our contemporaries, it is necessary to put it in systematic form. But we should never forget that to know and understand the system is not necessarily to know the experience, and that people can and do have the experience without ever being able to express it systematically.

CHAPTER

II

The Authority of the Bible

1. The Situation of the Bible Today

In the preceding chapter we said that by the term "Christianity" we mean Biblical Christianity. In the words of the Westminster Confession, "The Bible is the final authority for faith and practice." Most Prostestants still pay lip service to this statement, but, to put it mildly, they are baffled by the Bible and uncertain about what its authority really is. Year after year the Bible continues to be the best seller, but it is the most unread best seller. Except for the Christmas stories, the crucifixion stories, perhaps the Sermon on the Mount and a parable or two of Jesus', a few of the psalms and I Cor., ch. 13, multitudes of Christians know almost nothing about what is inside the covers of the Bible. They have no idea even of what it is to take the Bible as the authoritative "Word of God" speaking to them.

At no point has the intellectual revolution, which was briefly discussed at the beginning of the last chapter, had more devastating effects than in regard to the Bible. The Bible was written in a prescientific culture totally different from ours with a whole different world-view and set of assumptions about the nature of the natural world and about the relation (or lack of it) of cause and effect. The Bible was an easy target and the first casualty in the tragic war between science and religion which has raged for about one hundred years and only recently has begun to die down.

The Copernican revolution was bad enough, but the publication of Darwin's *Origin of Species* in 1859 was a body blow. As science went marching on to triumph after triumph, it convincingly demonstrated for all educated people that many of the claims of the Bible, taken literally as they are stated, simply are not true. For instance, if it can be said that we know anything, we know that our world has been in process for millions of years and was not created in six days in the year 4004 B.C. If the Bible is "wrong" in this and in many other incidents that it reports, for multitudes of people serious questions are raised as to its authority at other points. Added to the "attack from without" from science, there was, if anything, a more serious "attack from within" in the form of the work of Biblical scholarship which has critically examined how the Bible came to be written. Its results upset many applecarts. Its very method, namely, that the Bible could be critically examined by the scientific methods of historiography, was in itself a challenge to the sacredness of the Bible. We shall return to the questions implied in the "attack from without" and the "attack from within," which were both parts of the total intellectual revolution. Suffice it to say now that as a result of both of them the authority of the Bible was undermined. Since its authority was undermined, at least for most of the educated, it ceased to be read in any serious or Christian sense.

If Biblical Christianity is to be affirmed, it is obviously necessary to discover a way to read the Bible in the light of the established findings of modern science and of modern Biblical criticism and still hear it speaking as the authoritative Word of God. What follows is an attempt to show how this can be done.

2. Difficulties of Moderns with the Bible

At best the Bible is a difficult book to read. It is especially difficult for modern sophisticated and educated people who have been brought up in, and have often uncritically accepted, the contemporary scientific world-view (which is something different from the world-view of some of the best scientists). The Bible deals with the most fundamental problems of human existence but it deals with them, as we have noted, in terms of a culture, in fact several cultures and world-views, now long dead. Except for those who might well be called superstitious — those who take the Bible literally as a mysterious magic reference book — there is a double problem for most moderns. There is the problem of understanding at least something of the times and particular social milieu of a particular writer or story, and then the added problem of translating it so that it has meaning for our contemporary situation. This is not altogether easy. No great writing is altogether easy to understand. The Bible is no exception. But it can be understood by almost anyone who will make a little effort; and it is more than worth the effort.

Any book to be properly understood should be read from the point of view of the writer, and that certainly is true of the Bible. The Biblical writers were primarily, indeed exclusively, concerned with religion — with making known the ways of God to man. Consequently if the Bible is to be read aright, it must be read religiously. This is what is meant by saying that the Bible is the Word of God and that in it we hear God speak.

But what does it mean to read the Bible as the Word of God speaking to us, and how does one do it? The so-called Fundamentalists (they might more accurately be called literalists), who insist that every word was dictated by God and that the whole Bible must be taken literally, have an easy answer; but it is an answer that is pretty nearly impossible for educated people today. (Even these literalists, in spite of what they say, actually interpret, and they give more weight to some passages than they do to others.) Moreover, not only is there the fact that the Bible originated in a different world with a different cultural pattern where the scientific assumptions that we take for granted were unknown, there are also the obvious crudities. We may not actually be more moral than the ancients, but we do not, today, make a religious heroine of a woman who " gets her man " by seducing her father-in-law (Gen., ch. 38), or of another who, by waiting until her hoped-for husband is drunk, goes to bed at his feet (Ruth

3:6-10). In view of the conduct of modern warfare we are as brutal as ever, but we do not expect an acknowledged "man of God" to sacrifice his daughter for victory in battle (Judg. 11:29-40), nor to seize a sword and hack a bound and helpless former enemy "in pieces before the Lord" (I Sam. 15:32-33). It is not surprising that educated people today incredulously ask, "Can God really be speaking to me in stories like these?"

The "liberal" solution has been to point out that these stories and others like them, coming from a primitive period, represent a combination of historical fact and legend reflecting the culture and ethics of the time, but that there is a progressive evolutionary development in the Bible of man's understanding of both God and ethics. All this is true. As a result of modern Biblical research we know fairly well the circumstances under which most of the Bible was written, and we know that it was written over a period of more than a thousand years by many writers reflecting various points of view and degrees of insight. Ethically, from our point of view, some of these insights, particularly the earlier ones, seem pretty low. Unfortunately, however, the "liberal" viewpoint, while valuable up to a point, and while intellectually more respectable, has very serious dangers which the Fundamentalists have pointed out with some truth. Once this process is begun it is very difficult to know where to have it stop. In actual fact it ends in an anarchy of individual opinions in which the authority of the Bible to speak is determined almost entirely by how far it agrees with the relative opinions of the individual who has gotten his opinions from somewhere else — usually his own personal and cultural prejudices. The result is that the Bible ceases to be authoritative in any significant sense.

A further difficulty of the "liberal" approach is that, as a result of Biblical research, the layman finds it increasingly more difficult to know what is fact and what is fancy. If even the scholars debate some passages, how can the layman decide? This difficulty is just as great for the New Testament as it is for the Old. For instance, we know that none of the Gospels are factual biographies in the modern sense of the term; they were written from one to two or three generations after events they describe, and they represent the memories, traditions, and beliefs of the groups in which the particular writers lived. In this kind of situation even the teachings of Jesus tend to lose the certainty and therefore the authority they once had. To sift the wheat from the chaff becomes a lifetime study, and even then one cannot be sure of what he will get beyond recognition as a Biblical scholar — scarcely the reason for which the Bible was written! Most of the laity have neither time nor interest for this kind of study. It is not surprising, therefore, that today, when we so badly need it, there are multitudes, not only outside the churches but inside too, who know practically nothing about the Bible.

The sad thing is that there are many people who would like to return to the Bible, who feel that if they could only read it aright it would speak to them, but they do not know how to go about it. In order to maintain their intellectual integrity they cannot return to the literalism of the Fundamentalists, and the methods of the liberals seem to rob the Bible of all authority. As an attempt to get around these difficulties I would like to suggest some principles for Bible-reading that do not require giving up our intellectual integrity and that still enable us to hear the Bible speak as the Word of God.

3. Three Principles of Bible-Reading

The first principle is to recognize that some truths cannot be expressed literally and that to try to express them literally is to take the real meaning out of them. This attitude is somewhat difficult for mid-twentieth-century people, who are conditioned by a scientific, factually documented culture. But it is not impossible, and we still recognize this truth in the realm of the arts. All pictorial artists in order to give a "true" meaning to a picture employ deception. They use perspective. If an artist drew objects as they really exist, the picture would give an "untrue" impression. It may not be religiously insignificant that the present vogue in art is toward abstraction. To an art layman like myself, many of these abstract pictures are a combination of absurdity and laziness; but they also point to a new recognition that all truth cannot be comprehended in literal realism. In this respect abstractionism in art can be, at least religiously, healthy.

Be that as it may, something like the artistic method is one of the first requirements of Bible study. *To read the Bible seriously does not necessarily mean to read it literally*. It is well to remember that the Biblical writers, living in a culture different from ours, were happily not cursed with our literalism and exactitude. They were artists. They were essentially semi-Oriental storytellers, and they knew, as any good storyteller knows, particularly if he has a point to make, that making that point is more important than the details it is dressed in. If the point of the story can be made clearer and more compelling by inventing some details that did not happen, or even could not happen, that is not dishonesty; that is merely good and legitimate storytelling.

Such an understanding of the Bible stories, which I believe was the understanding of the writers themselves, can go a long way toward hearing the Bible speak without committing mental harakiri. For instance, the writer of Jonah, as a prescientific person, may have believed that a man could survive after being swallowed by a large fish, and again he may not have believed it. But he was not interested in that question and he would be dumfounded at the later discussion it created. He was simply adopting a vivid illustration to show the inescapableness of God. God is the creator of the whole world; he is not limited to one locality like Palestine and his providence extends everywhere. Even inside of a whale in the sea God operates! That is a point worth making! Again, the writer of John's Gospel, living in an age when everybody assumed miracles happened, probably never bothered his head about how water could instantly become wine. That question was the least important thing in the story he told of the marriage in Cana (John 2:1-11). The point he was making, and which the early Christians understood he was making, was that Christ is the "new wine" and that once a man has accepted, or "tasted," Christ everything he knew before is "flat" by comparison. Not only the writer of John but ten thousand times ten thousand Christians down through the ages have had a similar experience and know that it is true.

Thus, the Bible should be read seriously but not literally, and it is a pretty good rule of thumb that *the last and the least important question to ask about any given story is, "How could it have happened?"* This approach is particularly helpful in getting by the miracles, which are so difficult for moderns. The question of the miracles is a bigger one than can be fully dealt with here. In brief, miracles are certainly reported in the Bible and they were certainly believed by the early Christians. Some of the miracle stories have natural explanations and some do not. The miracles can provide a field day for arguments that get nowhere, particularly if one concentrates on the question, " How could they have happened? " But this is the wrong question to concentrate on, for certainly to the writers and to the early Christians the miracles reported were never ends in themselves; they were always used as pungent illustrations to point to a deeper, more significant meaning. John's Gospel, which particularly reports the miraculous, makes this clear when miracles are so often referred to as " signs." A sign always points to something beyond itself. This is true of miracles reported elsewhere too. When, for instance, at the death of our Lord, it says that " the curtain of the temple was torn in two, from top to bottom " (Matt. 27:51), the primary significance is not that if a person had gone to the Temple and looked at the curtain, which hid the Holy of Holies, he would see it torn in two. (The early Christians may or may not have believed that, but it is secondary.) The primary significance, which the writer of Matthew intended and which his readers understood, was that somehow, in Christ and in his death, the partition that separates sinful man from God (that is what the veil of the Temple did) had been destroyed, and that because of and through Christ's work on the cross a whole and new and direct relationship between man and God is now possible.

A second principle for reading the Bible is to recognize that *if God is going to speak to men in any meaningful fashion, he must speak to them in terms that they can understand, that is, in terms of their own experience.* For reasons that to him are good, God chose to speak to us through the writers of the Bible. This does not mean that God has not spoken to others through other people. The universality of the command to love our neighbor as ourself indicates that, and as Paul said, God has not anywhere left himself " without witness " (Acts 14:17). Inevitably God had to speak in terms that could be understood by those to whom he spoke. Consequently the " illustrations " or " forms " are always contemporary to the particular situation of the time. In this sense the evolutionary or developmental theory of the liberals has some validity. The ethical applications through which God could reveal his will to earlier and more primitive people would naturally be different and " lower " than they would be in later and more ethically sensitive periods. But again, as in the case of miracles, the applications are only illustrative of a deeper eternal principle. The job of the modern reader is not to let himself be distracted by the application but to go on to the principle involved and then apply it in terms of his own situation.

For instance, to take the four cases mentioned earlier: the stories of Tamar, Ruth, Jephthah, and Samuel. All of them are primitive and all of them involve actions we would condemn today. When one understands something of the customs of the times in which those ancients earned their bread and butter, their ethics are not nearly so shocking as they first appear, but that is more or less inconsequential. Their actions as actions are Biblically significant only because they illustrate a deeper principle. What is important is to get behind the particular acts to that principle and when we do we discover something that can be understood as the Word of God speaking to us even in the twentieth century. Each of these people, in his or her own way, did what he or she did because each believed that was what God required. Tamar believed that the law was God-given and that it demanded that her highest duty to both God and society was to raise up children for her dead husband (Deut. 25:5-10). She was even willing to sacrifice her virtue to be obedient to God's command. With

Ruth the situation is somewhat similar and her action was not as indiscreet then as it would be today. Also The Book of Ruth contains the larger idea, namely, that the grace of God can come to a foreigner (Ruth is a Moabitess, not a Hebrew); not an altogether bad point for mid-twentieth-century America. Jephthah had sworn an oath before God and he rightly recognized that not even family considerations justify breaking such an oath. It would be helpful today if we had a few more men in public office with Jephthah's discernment and integrity. In the rough-and-tough terms of Samuel's day the complete annihilation of an enemy was not considered inhuman; it was standard procedure. Samuel believed that God, who gave everything, had given the victory over the Amalekites. They therefore all belonged to him. To let one man go free, especially the king, was more than a lapse of rectitude, it was actually defiance of God and therefore blasphemy. Obedience to God demanded that he act as he did and he had the courage to be obedient in spite of what others might think.

The point behind each of these stories, which is illustrated in each story in a different but very human situation, is that God demands an obedience to his will (always understood in terms of the world in which we live), which goes beyond every other demand. When people obey this demand there is a price to pay — sometimes a very high price — but it is worth the price and the people are blest. This is not just an Old Testament conception; it is basic to the New Testament as well. Our Lord was "obedient unto death"; and Peter and John "must obey God rather than men"; Paul declares, "I was not disobedient to the heavenly vision." That this is a word that is needed today should be obvious to any thoughtful person. Our job is not to try to apply it in terms of a past culture, but to try to apply it in terms of our own contemporary life.

There is a third principle for Bible-reading and it is perhaps the most important of all. It is also for many people, at first glance, the most difficult to grasp. It is the principle that if one wants to get religious help from the Bible, he must go to it expecting religious help. *Faith speaks only to faith and the Bible speaks the*

Word of God only to those who go to it in faith and expectancy. The section on faith and reason in Chapter I has already dealt with the charge of wishful thinking which might be made here. As was recognized then, we are confronted here with a dilemma of human finiteness from which there is no perfect escape. No one, not even the most devout and intelligent Christian can avoid sometimes " getting out " what he is looking for. But this existential truth is not limited to people who take the Bible religiously. It is true of every area of life in which we seek meaning. Whether in art, or music, or even in the scientific laboratory, one discovers meaning only in so far as the person approaches the particular " object " in faith and expectancy.

This truth can perhaps be better illustrated from a more mundane area of life, in which more of us have had experience. In the area of courtship and marriage it is an odd thing that if a boy proposes to a girl and she does not love him, she will think he is funny. If she is a lady, she will be gentle and considerate in her refusal but she will still consider the whole business more or less absurd. The words of the suitor, " I love you," under these circumstances, if not actually ridiculous, are at least meaningless. But if the girl loves the boy too, then he is no longer ridiculous; he is wonderful! And the very same words, " I love you," which in the first case were funny and meaningless, in the second case become freighted with glorious, life-enriching meaning. The difference is not in the words said — they are the same words — the difference is in the answering faith and expectancy.

It is ever thus. In all areas of life as well as in Bible-reading it is a condition of human existence which must be accepted. Needless to say, awareness of the inherent dangers of this inescapable human characteristic should make us move with considerable caution. Particularly, in important matters that have consequence for other people, the serious Bible reader will want to check his findings with those of other serious Bible readers and with the historic experience preserved in the Christian fellowship which is the Church. But with these checks the risk must be run — and when run, we find we have not run in vain.

4. The Authority of the Bible

These principles, I think, if taken seriously, can go a long way toward helping us to read the Bible meaningfully in the twentieth century, and also they illustrate what it means to read the Bible as authoritative. We have just seen that of all the principles for Bible-reading the most important is that it be read in faith, but as was pointed out in the preceding chapter, Christian faith cannot be a blind faith, " believing what you know ain't so." Faith too must be so grounded in our practical experience that its claims make sense to us as we go along through life. As this necessity relates itself to the question of the Bible it means that the authority of the Bible does not rest on an external authority. We Biblical Christians do not believe that the Bible is " the final authority for faith and practice " because the Westminster Confession says it is. Neither do we accept the authority of the Bible because the minister, or the Church, or a church council tells us we must. We accept the authority of the Bible because, and only because, when we read it seriously, trying to find the meaning of what it says to us, we find it does " speak to our condition." It tells us the truth, sometimes unpleasant truth that we would rather not hear, about ourselves and our lives as we have to live them in our kind of world. This is the only law there is for establishing the authority of the Bible.

The rest of this book is an attempt to illustrate and make cogent this thesis. It is an attempt to present the major Biblical Christian affirmations in such a way as to show what they mean and how they answer the fundamental problems of life. But before we turn to those affirmations, one further word about Bible-reading needs to be said.

In order really to grasp — or, better, be grasped by — the Biblical point of view, it requires something far more disciplined than just casual, piecemeal reading. The Bible is not a magic-formula book. The idea that you can go to it in a random fashion and find the answer to any particular problem is not Christian. Christian Bible-reading demands serious, regular, disciplined reading of blocks large enough to give some continuity and small enough to be digested. Essentially to read the Bible so that it becomes the authoritative Word of God speaking to us means to read it over and over again until the whole Biblical point of view gradually seeps into our systems, until we find that unconsciously we have so absorbed its general point of view that without really thinking about it we meet life's questions and make our decisions in terms of it.

CHAPTER

III

God

THE BIBLE NEVER OFFERS AN ARGUMENT FOR THE EXISTENCE OF GOD; it simply assumes his existence. Furthermore, the Bible never describes God. It relates that when Moses wanted to know God's name (names in the Bible are essentially descriptive) God replied, "I AM WHO I AM" (Ex. 3:14). As Thomas Browne observed, "'I AM WHO I AM' was his own definition unto Moses; and it was a short one to confound mortality that durst question God, or ask him who he was."[6] The Bible tells of God's activity as revealed to men — he creates, judges righteously, forgives, redeems, loves, directs history, and so on — but God himself is never defined. Even in Isaiah's vision God is not actually seen, for "the house was filled with smoke" (Isa. 6:4). Indeed, the Bible lays down strict prohibitions against trying to describe God. It states specifically, "For man shall not see me and live" (Ex. 33:20). And the Decalogue is emphatic: "You shall not make yourself a graven image, or any likeness of anything that is in heaven above, or that is in the earth beneath, or that is in the water under the earth; you shall not bow down to them or serve them; for I the Lord your God am a jealous God" (Ex. 20:4-5).

The Bible here shows a wisdom that goes beyond human wisdom, and that is one reason why we speak of the Bible as "the Word of God." God in his totality is beyond finite human comprehension; we can understand him only as he makes himself known to us. If God could be comprehended in his totality and captured in any "graven image," he would not be God, but instead he would be something less even than man. The Bible profoundly recognizes this fact and declares that every "graven image" or "idol," no matter how well intentioned or how well conceived, is the product of man's thinking and making. It is something less than God, or something other than God and therefore a blasphemous distortion of God!

Although today, at least in Christianity, we do not make physical idols or graven images of God (neither do the Jews nor the Mohammedans, who are rooted in the Old Testament), this Biblical prohibition still has a direct word to say to our times. The graven images against which the law of Moses originally protested were idols made of wood and stone which were intended by their makers to be representations of God. They were made sincerely as the best that men could devise, but the Bible recognized that they were not good enough — in fact, they were blasphemous. Today we do not make idols out of wood and stone, but we do make them out of our philosophical systems and our ideologies. It is very important to remember that a philosophical description of God can be just as much of a human representation as a physically graven image can be; it is just as much the product of human devising and is thereby just as much a blasphemous distortion. (Much of honest atheism arises from a genuine, although frequently unconscious, recognition that what some people too easily describe as God cannot be God, or at least any god the honest atheist can accept.) As Paul said, "The world did not know God through wisdom." (I Cor. 1:21.)

> "Claiming to be wise, they became fools, and exchanged the glory of the immortal God for images resembling mortal man or birds or animals or reptiles.
>
> "Therefore God gave them up in the lusts of their hearts. . . , because they exchanged the truth about God for a lie and worshiped and served the creature rather than the Creator, who is blessed forever! Amen." (Rom. 1:22-25.)

This Scripture applies not only to idols in the original sense but also to idols in the sense of philosophical systems and ideologies.

An acquaintance of mine once observed: " A man must worship either God or his own mind. It must be one or the other; it cannot be both! " At first this seems to be a harsh and extreme statement, but on further examination it is seen to be true. In the last analysis and in actual fact, all men must say either that " my mind is supreme and any conception of God must submit to the dictates of my thinking," or else that " God is supreme and I must submit my thinking to him even if I do not understand him completely." It is the inevitable tragedy of all ideologies and philosophical systems, even those that claim to be theistic, that they tend to take the former position, and, in so far as they are accepted as adequate descriptions of God or of ultimate reality, they thereby become idols against which the Bible rightly protests.

The importance of this Biblical prohibition cannot be overestimated, especially in a consideration of philosophical arguments for and descriptions of God. It is inevitable, in order to think about God at all, that we employ conceptions and that they be logically derived, but, at best, they are only symbolical pointers and partial statements. All of them are something less than God. To say that God is " The Principle or Concretion," or " The Pure Mathematician," or " The Process," or " Wholeness," and so forth, may say something about God's activity, but to say that God *is* any one of these is to reduce God blasphemously and to say something very different from what is revealed in the Bible.

Thus, at best, philosophical systems, Christianly speaking, are very deceptive. Most colleges offer one or more courses in the philosophy of religion. Were I a college president, I should keep such a course in the curriculum, for it can be an excellent intellectual discipline, and when there is already a predisposition to believe in God, it can be very helpful. Strictly speaking, however, from the Christian point of view a course in the philosophy of religion is a contradiction of terms. Philosophy, if it is good philosophy and true to itself, must of necessity limit itself to what the human mind can know as deduced from the world by the rational empirical method. It is properly the pursuit of truth as the human reason can grasp it. Biblical religion, as was noted in the preceding chapter, is not the pursuit of truth; rather, it is the declaration of truth already revealed by God. The two are as different as chalk and cheese, and to try to make Biblical religion fit into the assumptions and categories of philosophy is, as we have also seen, to put it in an impossible position. It is like judging the color yellow in terms of the color blue. Consequently it is not surprising that the products of our philosophy of religion courses, as far as Christian understanding is concerned, turn out a little green.

The philosophical arguments for the existence of God do not prove that God exists. If they did, all reasonable and intelligent people would believe in him. The simple fact is that many very intelligent people do not believe in God, at least not consciously in any Christian sense. Belief in God is not primarily the result of philosophical argument; it is primarily the result of faith and of the experience of the grace of God. Nevertheless, once there is a predisposition on the part of the individual to believe, philosophy can perform a valuable critical function and the philosophical arguments can be very helpful supports for that belief. From an intelligent point of view, they do make the probability of God seem more probable. Therefore, for the sake of record, I shall outline briefly the major philosophical arguments for God.

1. The Philosophical Arguments for God

One of the oldest arguments, going at least as far back as Aristotle, is the *causal argument*. This argument is based on the thesis that everything that happens has an antecedent cause, but that an infinite regression of causes is a meaningless term. We can say that A was caused by B and B was caused by C and so on, but an infinite list of causes becomes unthinkable. We must stop somewhere, if not at Z, at Z^1, or Z^{10}, in order to start thinking. Somewhere along the line it is necessary to posit a first cause. When this theory is applied to our existence we can push it back and back through the geologic ages to the beginning of our world and universe (however scientists describe and date that event) and ask, What caused that? Since this is about as far as the mind can go, and an infinite regression of causes is meaningless, the answer often given is that there was a first cause, an uncaused cause, or prime mover, which is God. Objectors to this argument claim that logically an endless regression of causes is no more unthinkable than an uncaused cause. On a strictly logical and rational ground it would be hard to say which of the two is more thinkable or unthinkable. The answer any particular person makes will probably be made on a basis of subjective preference already determined on other grounds as to whether one believes or disbelieves in God. The most that can be said for the causal argument is that if there is a predisposition to believe in God it gives some support to that belief. However, it should be noted that the God who is just a first cause is considerably less than the God of the Christian faith.

A second argument for the existence of God is the argument from *design,* or the *cosmological argument.* Men have long noted that within the flux, variety, and even confusion of life and of the cosmos there appears to be a certain magnificent orderliness. In the physical world night and day follow each other regularly; the laws of gravitation operate uniformly; the stars move according to known laws; and the same elements, in about the same proportion, that are found on our earth are found in the outer planets, the sun, and even in the most distant stars. In the living world that we know there is a remarkable balance between plant and animal life. Even death and decay have their place (without them the world would soon be so cluttered up that life would be impossible) and Thoreau could rightly rejoice in the stench of a dead horse because it revealed that nature, or nature's God, was on the job. All of this amazing balance has led many thoughtful people to think that the least rational conclusion to draw from this amazing orderliness is that it all happened by accident—or by a series of happy accidents. They have said that such an amazingly intricate design must be the work of a mind, of a designer, who can be called God. The chief illustration of this argument is the famous watch illustration. If a man found, in the woods, a fine watch, delicately balanced and in perfect running order, the most logical conclusion would be, not that the parts had accidentally collected themselves and started running, but rather that someone had made the watch and started it running. In like manner, the most intelligent conclusion to draw from the complexity and order of the cosmos is that there is a master designer, God.

A further extension of the argument from design is what is known as the *teleological argument,* or the argument from *purpose.* Perhaps the universe, but certainly the earth and especially our life upon it, reveals not only a kind of static design like a watch; it also reveals a kind of development that appears to have a direction or purpose. This argument has received its greatest support from the theory of evolution. However our earth started, it seems first to have been a lifeless molten ball which gradually cooled, attracted moisture, and then somehow developed life. Through millions of years this life which began, presumably, in unicellular forms, developed into multicellular forms, and gradually there evolved fishes, reptiles, birds, mammals, and at last man with his strange spiritual needs and possibilities. All of this development, which from the human point of view is from the lower to the higher, seems to indicate, not only that there is a design, but also, that the design is one of growth, that it is going somewhere; in a word, that the design has a purpose. The most adequate explanation to account for this apparent purpose is that there is a purposeful God who is behind it all.

The first three arguments all rest primarily on the observation of the natural world and conclusions drawn from it. The next three arguments depend more particularly on an analysis of the strictly human situation and are a little more abstract.

One of these is the *ontological argument* and it was given its classic expression by Saint Anselm. In a way, the ontological argument is related to the causal argument, for it assumes a relationship between essence and existence. As this argument goes, we all have an idea of a perfect being than which nothing greater nor more perfect can be conceived. This Being must exist or else we could not have an idea of it, and this Being is God. As Anselm made clear when Gaunilo pointed out that it was possible to have an idea of a perfect island that did not exist, his (Anselm's) argument did not apply to arbitrary notions but only to those which are necessarily conceived or absolute. Descartes modified this somewhat by saying that I have an idea of a perfect and infinite being but I am imperfect and finite, therefore I could not have the idea unless it had reality outside of me. Or, as J. S. Whale has put it, "The very idea of God is possible to us only because God already stands behind it."[7] It is impossible to have an idea of nothing, for the moment a person has an idea of nothing he gives the nothing a being and an existence. Therefore, so this argument runs, atheism is really a negative affirmation of God because in order to deny God he must first be affirmed. Thus, God is "The-Ground-of-Existence" and "That-Which-Makes-Existence-Possible"; he is the presupposition of the possibility of all thinking. That is why Anselm made his famous statement, "I believe in order that I may understand."

A fifth philosophical argument is the argument of *idealism*. In one form or another it is very ancient, going back at least as far as Plato, but in modern times the *idealistic argument* for God is usually associated with Bishop Berkeley. It is based on the assumption of the complete subjectivity of all knowledge. The knowledge that any man has comes to him through the operation of one of the five senses — seeing, hearing, feeling, smelling, tasting. Each of these senses when sensitized is really only a reaction in the mind, or the brain, of the individual. Thus, all knowledge is always completely subjective; it is always a process going on within the individual and there is no absolute proof that what one person says he knows is the same as what another person says he knows. For instance, when you and I see a lawn we may agree that it is green but there is no way to prove that you and I see the same color. It may simply be that from infancy we have both been taught to associate the name green with the color reaction we receive upon seeing a lawn. Nothing can be proved to exist except as it exists in someone's mind, in which case it does not exist objectively at all.

On the basis of pure logic and rational analysis it is hard to see how this position can be refuted, for all that we know about the objective world does in fact end as nothing more than impressions in the minds of persons. On the other hand, it also is a fact of experience that objects do appear to have an objective reality. The classic illustration is that of a tree. Can it be said that a tree continues to exist if there is no one to perceive it? The logical answer on the basis of the subjectivity of all knowledge is, "No." Yet the simple fact remains that every time anyone comes to the spot where the tree is—there it is! One man can describe it to a stranger and the stranger can find it. It appears to have an objective reality independent of men's minds. How can this conflict be resolved? Berkeley's answer is that the tree and all other objects in the phenomenal world have an independent existence and an objective reality because they are constantly held (thought, observed) in the Universal Mind, the mind of God. It is the mind of God which gives the world objective reality. The whole idealistic argument has been put succinctly in two limericks:

The Question

There was a young man who said: "God
Must find it exceedingly odd,
    If he finds that this tree
    Continues to be
When there's no one about in the Quad."

The Answer

Dear Sir,
        Your astonishment's odd!
I am always about in the Quad!
    And that's why the tree
    Will continue to be
Since observed by,
                Yours faithfully,
                    God.

A sixth argument is the *moral argument,* with which the name of Immanuel Kant is associated. Not all men agree on what constitutes good and moral action. What constitutes good morality in one time and culture may be quite different from the standard in another time and culture, and even within a given culture there are variations. Often what some men call good others call bad. For instance, today we, in the democratic societies, believe it is good to have a high regard for the individual and that it is bad to sacrifice the individual to the state, but in fascist and communist societies it is good to sacrifice the individual to the state and it is bad to place the needs of the individual above those of the state. (These and other variations in ethics are what has led some people to deny that there is an absolute morality and to defend moral and ethical relativity.) However, in all these conflicting ideas which men have held and still do hold about what is moral, one fact stands out, namely: *all men everywhere have some standard of what is good and what is bad*. What one group may think good may be the opposite of what another group thinks good, but there never has been a society, or even an individual, without some sense of good and bad. Even the most degraded criminal has some sense of moral consciousness, moral responsibility, "oughtness" or "duty," if only of a very low criminal standard. In other words, the sense of moral consciousness, or "oughtness," appears to be a universal human characteristic. How can this situation be explained? The answer given by Kant is that it can be explained only on the assumption that there is a moral lawgiver — God. The advantage of this argument, if true, over the others is that it adds something immeasurably precious to the idea of God. Not only is God a first cause and a purposeful designer, or mind, but God is also moral and his purpose is a moral purpose.

These six philosophical arguments for God, outlined all too inadequately, have played an important role in the history of Christian thought, philosophy, and theology. But again it must be emphasized that no one of them, nor even all of them put together, can claim to *prove* that God is. Writes Paul Tillich:

"There can be little doubt that the arguments are a failure in so far as they claim to be arguments. . . . The arguments for the existence of God are neither arguments nor are they proof of the existence of God. They are expressions of the *Question* of God which is implied in human finitude. This question is their truth; every answer they give is untrue."[8]

The philosophical arguments are not proofs because at the level of argument it is always rationally possible for a person to say, "I do not believe it," and no one can prove him wrong. As a matter of fact, an uncaused cause is no more thinkable than an infinite regression of causes. Both are beyond human comprehension. Strictly speaking logical reason does not necessarily require the assumption of a designer or even a mind. The whole universe and the whole human enterprise may be just an accident, or a series of "happy" accidents. Even the appearance of moral purpose, if granted, can be explained on the basis of the laws of the survival of the fitter. Given enough time (and if the geologists are right, there has been plenty of time), the laws of evolution working by chance can explain everything. As someone has said: "Ten million monkeys typing on ten million typewriters for ten million years could, by accident, produce all the works of Shakespeare." Such a statement seems to me a little absurd but until ten million monkeys have pounded typewriters for ten million years it cannot be proved false.

The philosophical arguments do not prove God, but if, as I have said, there is a predisposition to believe, even if there is a willingness to entertain the possibility that there may be a God, then the arguments, particularly their cumulative testimony, do give a strong support. They make belief not less rational than disbelief. But faith must come first and does come first. (The willingness to examine the evidence favorably is itself an act of faith.)

One further negative observation needs to be made about these philosophical arguments. Even if a person, because of a conscious or unconscious predisposition to believe, finds them convincing, the God to whom they point falls far short of the God of Christian faith. They point to a God of power, and of purpose, and of wisdom, perhaps even a God of moral purpose, but they do not point to a God who loves, forgives, and redeems ordinary men and women caught in all the complex difficulties of human existence. Kant, in elaborating his moral argument, thought he was defending Christianity from its attackers (particularly David Hume), but it is debatable whether or not he rendered a greater disservice than a service. Anyone who argues from the God of the philosophers to the God incarnated in Jesus Christ, " who, though he was in the form of God, . . . emptied himself, taking the form of a servant. . . . And being found in human form he humbled himself and became obedient unto death, even death on a cross " (Phil. 2:6-8), makes a jump of faith which cannot be logically drawn from the arguments. The God who has revealed himself in Jesus Christ is known only through faith and through the experience of faith.

One of the difficulties of so many people, when it comes to the question of God, particularly in our matter-of-fact culture, is that they want " God tied up in a neat package " and explained in precise terms. They tend to want to think of God as Something or Somebody, or at least as some Being that can be precisely defined. As the Bible makes clear, this is impossible, and as long as a person persists in such an attitude he will be unable to know the God who is really God. Emil Brunner says that for anyone who asks the question, " Is there a God? " silence is the only answer possible.[9] The question, " Is there a God? " states the question the wrong way, for it assumes that God is a thing, or a being, like other things such as a mountain, or a house, or a person. This is just what God is not, as we have seen when Moses received the enigmatic answer, " I AM WHO I AM." Speaking via Deutero-Isaiah, God says precisely, " I am God and there is none else; I am God, and there is none like me " (Isa. 46:9). In other words, God is not to be thought of as a thing or being like anything else. The importance of this cannot be overestimated. Paul Tillich inveighs against the " thingification of God," [10] and Eric Frank writes that even " existence is a category much too inferior to be applied to the greatness of God." [11]

On this basis it looks at first as though we ought to give up trying to say anything about God beyond the old deacon's definition of God as "an oblong blur," and call off the whole inquiry. On rational empirical grounds alone this attitude is probably correct; it is only by faith in the Biblical revelation that we can say anything positive about God. Dr. Herbert Spiegelberg, in a provocative article in the *Journal of Philosophy and Science,* points out that even the statements of the theologians about God are negative statements when critically examined from a strictly rational philosophical point of view; "even the analogical attributes of Divinity are primarily, if not exclusively, negative attributes." [12] On the basis of Dr. Spiegelberg's rationalistic assumptions I believe he is right.

Certainly any philosophic attempt to define God, if it is to have any truth, must include in it the affirmation that God, in himself, is beyond human comprehension. In order to think and communicate at all we must use language and definitions, but any definition of God must point to his indefinableness if it is to be a good definition. Thus, the definition of Rudolf Otto that God is the *Mysterium Tremendum* (Mysterious Tremendousness) and the definition "Wholly Other" have some validity.[13] Other definitions that fulfill this requirement are "The-Ground-of-Existence" and "That-Which-Makes-Existence-and-Thinking-Possible." God is too great for human understanding except as he has revealed himself to faith. As J. S. Whale says after listing the philosophical arguments for God: "But who God is, God himself must tell us in revelation or we shall never know. Revelation means a dynamic self-disclosure on the part of the Other to which man responds by faith." [14]

We cannot prove by the rational empirical method that God exists, but we believe through faith that God is the Ground of all existence and the beginning point of all thinking. We cannot say philosophically what God is except that he is the Wholly Other, but by faith we believe that he has revealed enough of himself (primarily in Jesus Christ) for our need, and within the context of faith and revelation verified by Christian experience, we can say all those things about God which are necessary for human living—that is all that is necessary!

In the next chapter we shall consider more fully the nature of man. For the moment it is enough to say that all men are primarily concerned with living what they believe to be the good life. In actual fact achieving the good life is a precarious proposition filled with disappointments and frustrations. And as has been pointed out before, everything we think or do is thought or done from the human point of view. This is a condition of our human finiteness. In this sense religion is valuable only as it enhances human living (which includes dying). All men practice whatever religion they profess because they believe it helps them to meet the difficulties of human existence. Religion must be of use to men or else it is of no use at all. (This does not mean that religion is simply the invention of men, as has sometimes been said; rather, religion in general and Christianity in particular are correct responses to the fundamental human situation as given by God.) It is the claim of Christianity, as the final revelation of God, that it meets the actual needs of men and women in their struggles with the problems of human living. On that claim Christianity stands or falls. Christianity asserts that there is a God who is the creator of all existence and that consequently if men are to live at their best they must live in terms of that God. Further, Christianity claims that God has revealed enough of himself, his will, and his intentions for man, most fully in Jesus Christ, so that men can fulfill the demands of God and realize their most creative selves. We do not need to know all about God, nor do we need to be able to describe him completely. It is not necessary for us to know God's plans for Arcturus and whatever satellites may be around it, nor his intentions for mosquitoes. All we need to know are God's intentions regarding man, and his nature as it affects our human lives. We have that most fully in his revelation, which is called the Christian religion.

2. The Trinity

It is axiomatic that if there is a God who is Wholly Other and unknown to man except as he reveals himself, such revelations as he may make to men must be in terms of human experience and in terms men can understand. Christianity therefore speaks of God as Trinitarian.

Strictly speaking, the Bible does not mention the Trinity as such, and in the New Testament there are only three passages that have the Trinitarian formula. One is I John 5:7 in the King James Version: "For there are three that bear record in heaven, the Father, the Word, and the Holy Ghost: and these three are one." This verse is not found in all the most ancient manuscripts and today it is regarded as not genuine. The new Revised Standard Version does not give it even in a footnote. A second is Paul's benediction found in II Cor. 13:14: "The grace of the Lord Jesus Christ and the love of God and the fellowship of the Holy Spirit be with you all." According to *The Interpreter's Bible,* "this verse is not a formal statement of the doctrine of the Trinity, but it reflects the aspects of divine redemption and Christian experience which led the church later to formulate the doctrine."[15] A third is in Matt. 28:19: "Go therefore and make disciples of all nations, baptizing them in the name of the Father and of the Son and of the Holy Spirit." Most scholars agree with Peake that "the command to baptize in the threefold name is a late doctrinal expansion."[16] Actually the doctrine of the Trinity did not become fully established until the Council of Nicaea in 325.

Nevertheless, the Trinity has become a central rallying point for the Christian faith in defense of itself against its attackers and modifiers. And the formula is implicit in the Bible, more especially in the New Testament, but also in the Old Testament in its predictions of the coming Messiah. The Bible speaks of God's self-revelation to men in three ways: the activity of the Father Creator, the activity of the Son, and the activity of the Holy Spirit or Holy Ghost. It was inevitable that Christians, as they expressed this threefold revelation in their lives, and as they tried to defend their faith against Greek philosophical abstractions on the one hand and pagan polytheism on the other, should develop the doctrine of the Trinity.

Nonetheless, this doctrine creates some confusion in the minds of many people because they wrongly think of it as some kind of impossible proposition or Chinese puzzle, about three people being one person. The doctrine of the Trinity is nothing more or less than an attempt, within the limitations of human language and thought, to express how we experience God's self-revelation of himself in terms of the human situation. Considered in this light, two factors emerge. One is the unity of God; the other is the variety, even ambiguity of the human situation. The Trinity tries to express these. On the one hand it declares the unity of God: God as revealed in the Father, and in the Son, and in the Holy Spirit is always the same God. It is something like looking at a mountain from three different sides. Each view presents a different understanding but it is always the same mountain. On the other hand, because of the ambiguity of the life men actually live, it is inevitable that God must make himself known in a variety of ways. Thus, in a sense it is correct to say that the primary function of the Trinity is to express symbolically the unity of God as revealed in the variety of human life. As such it is the most realistic understanding of God there is. It is perhaps significant that in one high non-Christian religion, Hinduism, there are indications of the Trinity; however, as A. J. Toynbee points out, the Hindu trinity of Brahma, Vishnu, and Siva never becomes a real unity and thereby it loses power.[17]

Without going into an elaborate discussion of the problem of knowledge, it is fair to say that all knowledge any man has comes to him in one of three ways. Some of our knowledge comes to us as a result of the observation of natural phenomena — we learn from our experience in contact with the natural world. Some of our knowledge, perhaps most of it, comes from other people — parents, teachers, and others; even the books we read were written by someone. Some of our knowledge comes from our own reflection on the phenomena of the world and on what we learn from people. In such reflections we sometimes get an insight of meaning which gives a new understanding. A story is told of the late Thomas Edison: It seems that someone said to him, "Mr. Edison, what tremendous inspiration you must have had!" To this Mr. Edison replied, "Ninety-nine per cent perspiration and one per cent inspiration!" Mr. Edison's reply was probably correct, but it was the one per cent of inspiration that made the ninety-nine per cent of perspiration succeed. In a word, we learn also by insight, intuition, and inspiration.

These are the three ways by which we learn. It is normal expectancy that if there is a God who wishes to communicate himself to men for their welfare, he should use the methods whereby men understand and learn.

One of the ways, then, we learn about God (or more properly speaking in Christian terms, one of the ways by which God reveals himself to us) is through the observation of the natural world. Everything that is created has the marks of its creator upon it. If there is a God who created this world, then, in the processes of nature, in the succession of seasons, in the organization of the stars and the atoms, in the laws of life and death, and so on, it is most logical to believe that we have revelations of God. Since Christianity begins with the assumption of God, it claims that, to faith, God has revealed himself in the natural world as creator. It is the recognition of this truth that gives such validity as there is to all forms of naturalism—God *is* revealed in the natural world. Thus we speak of God as creator. In fact, Christianity speaks of *creatio ex nihil,* that God created out of nothing. "In the beginning God created the heavens and the earth." (Gen. 1:1.) (In this sense Christianity rejects evolution as a *final* cause. The theory of evolution may and probably does describe the *method* by which God developed the world to its present state. Certainly today the evolutionary theory, as an explanation for the way in which the world reached its present state, is so successful that it is past dispute. To accept evolution in this sense, however, is something quite different from saying it is the final explanation.) Since man with his reason, his imagination, and his concern for values is also part of the created world, the Creator is revealed as not merely a prime mover, nor a mechanical law, nor impersonal will. God must also include in his nature that which makes human personality possible. Thus the Apostles' Creed rightly speaks of " God the *Father* Almighty, Maker of heaven and earth." The term " Father " includes creativity and personality. However, other attributes of the term " Father," such as love, forgiveness, and guidance, are derived more from God's revelation in the Second Person than from the First Person of the Trinity.

The idea of God as creator, in Biblical terms, includes further the recognition that God is the creator of history. The question of the Christian interpretation of history will be discussed later. For the moment, except for Zoroastrianism,[18] Biblical religion alone has a sense of historical destiny. (Modern doctrines of progress are secular corruptions of the Biblical conception.) The Bible sees history as part of the created order and therefore also as revealing something of God's intentions. Finally, the assertion that God is Creator means that he is the Ground of all being and existence, and that as such he is the primary fact of data and the beginning point from which everything else must be understood.

In all these ways we learn about God from the natural world and we speak of God as revealed in the natural world, as, " God the Father Almighty, Maker of heaven and earth," the First Person of the Trinity.

It is perhaps easiest to see God in the marvelous manifestations of nature. At least many people seem to feel most aware of God in a beautiful sunset or in majestic scenery. It is significant that in primitive religions one form or another of nature worship predominates; the instinct among primitive peoples which makes them respond to the mystery and manifestations of nature is a true instinct. In this sense primitive nature worship is an early preparation for later fuller revelations. God does reveal himself in nature. But the revelation in nature is not all of God, nor is it enough from a Christian, or even a human, point of view. As the God of nature, God is revealed as a God of power and majesty, but he is not revealed in nature as concerned with ordinary individual people, especially not as loving, forgiving, and redeeming them. Nature, except that it makes life possible, is largely indifferent to the aspirations of the human spirit. Our nature enthusiasts frequently forget that the God they worship in the sunset and in the harvest is the same God who produces the tornado and the drought! To see God only, or even primarily, in nature is to see a God of awe-inspiring majesty but one who is ethically indifferent to human individuals caught in the complex problems of living. The God of nature alone is a half-God and therefore a pagan God; were we left with this revelation alone, we should still be in paganism. Fortunately, however, God, out of his infinite mercy and wisdom, has not left us with the single revelation of himself found in nature. There is a second way to learn about God — from persons and especially from a Person.

Since man's life, while obviously part of the natural world, also has aspects that transcend his physical needs and point to elements that cannot be fulfilled completely in terms of the natural world, it is normal expectancy that God should reveal himself in ways beyond natural revelation and which meet these spiritual needs of men. Christianity claims that God has done this in Jesus of Nazareth who is the Christ. In making this unique claim for Jesus Christ, Christianity does not claim that he is the *only* revelation of God. In the saints, seers, and sages of all ages, and particularly in the patriarchs and prophets of the Hebrew people (especially chosen for reasons known only to God), we learn something of God. Indeed, all of us who are Christians today have learned about God and about Jesus Christ from someone — or ones — most of whom would not be classified as either saints or sages. In Jesus Christ, however, there is an *unique* revelation. All other revelations must be judged in terms of him to be genuine, either as preparation for receiving his revelation or as later applications of it. Jesus Christ is God's unique self-revelation, his incarnation in human history. As such, Jesus Christ is called the Second Person of the Trinity; he reveals infinitely more of God's intentions regarding man than we obtain from the First Person alone. In Chapter V, we shall consider the significance of Christ more fully, but for the moment it is from him and him alone that we learn of God's suffering love and redeeming forgiveness. This is not a negation of the revelation of the First

Person; it simply adds immeasurably to it.

It is good to know that there is a God who is the creator of all there is and "whose purposes falter not, neither are stayed"; it is good to know that once in his infinite wisdom God incarnated himself in a man for our salvation. Because of this knowledge we are infinitely richer and can meet the problems of life far more courageously. Nevertheless, we live, actually, in a hard world full of frustrations, and because we are weak it is difficult and often impossible to follow Christ completely. We are called upon to make hard decisions on which depend not only our own welfare but often the welfare of those we love, or for whom we are responsible. There is no sure rule. The question, "Just exactly what is the will of God for me in this particular situation?" can be a very difficult question to answer and one on which the best advice we secure often conflicts. What to do? The God revealed in nature seems distant and impersonal; the God revealed in Jesus Christ seems a long way off in another culture and giving only general principles. Christian faith, speaking from its own existential experience, declares that in such situations God has not left us helpless and alone. The earnest, faithful seeker, through prayer and worship and through interpreting circumstance, finds guidance in the midst of life and finds courage to make decisions and face life realistically. All of this indicates God's continuing self-revelations. We call this self-revelation the work of the Holy Spirit, the Third Person of the Trinity.

In the history of Christian thought and in the Bible there is some ambiguity as to the exact relationship between the Holy Spirit and God and Christ. At times the Holy Spirit seems to be considered primarily as an expression of the Father, and at times primarily as an expression of the Son. At times Christians speak of the leading and guidance of God, at times of the spirit or indwelling presence of Christ, at times simply of the work of the Holy Spirit. This ambiguity should not disturb us; it arises naturally from the ambiguity of the human situation and man's inability to comprehend God completely. All these expressions are attempts to put into language a fact of Christian experience, namely, that there is a third way in which we learn from God, here and now, in the midst of our daily living.

Thus, the three so-called Persons of the Trinity are seen as symbolic expressions of the three ways by which we know anything. The symbol "Person" is used because each of the three revelations is a revelation to persons and therefore must have an element of personality in it. At the significant levels of human experience, the levels at which Christianity operates, persons can only communicate with persons. Yet actually there is only one God, and, as mentioned above, the first function of the Trinity is to insist on the unity of God. The Father, the Son, and the Holy Spirit are all symbolical descriptions of the self-revelation of the same God. And each is necessary for a full understanding; if any one is left out we have something less than a full understanding. If God the Father Almighty, the Creator, is eliminated, the whole basis of religion and the possibility of giving meaning to life is destroyed; if God the Son is eliminated, the unique meaning of Christianity with its gospel of love, redemption, and hope is destroyed; if God the Holy Spirit is eliminated, all possibility for continuing personal and social growth and development is destroyed. The Trinity alone answers the fundamental question implied in the God-man relationship.

3. Other Characteristics of God

As was stated at the beginning of this chapter, the Bible expressly forbids the making of graven images or the describing of God. Nevertheless, human life and thought being what they are, it is necessary to have designations for God that describe some of his attributes, if not God himself, in order that men can talk and think about him at all. This creates a problem: namely, how to describe what cannot be described, and, how can what cannot be named be communicated? The ancient Hebrews solved this problem ingeniously. Their name for God was "Yahweh," which has been rather badly translated in our older English Bibles as "Jehovah." The word "Yahweh," however, was never to be mentioned. It was the ineffable name, too sacred for human lips to utter. The Hebrews had for convenience another less sacred name, "Adonai" (Lord), which could be used; and inevitably as they thought about their relation to God they used other terms to help clarify God's self-revelation. The Bible speaks of God as Lord, as Judge, as Holy, as Love, as Providential, and so on. In addition to the terms used in the Trinitarian formula all of these are still used. They need a brief word of explanation.

First of all, none of these terms, nor all of them together, are intended to be complete and final descriptions of God. Rather, all of them are merely attempts of men to describe in one way or another their various experiences of God's revelation. And all of them presuppose a Creator who is the Master of his creation.

The term *Lord* is obviously borrowed from the human social situation of a more primitive time than ours when a lord (*baal*) had absolute and undisputable right over all he possessed, including all human beings. Today we use the term "lord" too easily and it has lost most of its content for moderns. In the Biblical world no man called another "lord" unless, either from loyalty or from fear, he was ready to submit and acknowledge that the one called "lord" had absolute power to determine his life in all its phases and to determine even whether he should live or die. The Bible speaks of the relation between God (or Christ) and his people as a Lord-slave relationship. Unfortunately modern translation tends to render the word "slave" as "bond-servant," which in our time has become much less significant than what was originally meant. In the Bible, God (and in the New Testament, Christ) is Lord, with all the rights over man which a lord had over his slave. On the basis of the Biblical faith this use of the term "lord" is correct. If God is the creator of all there is, then he must be Lord in this absolute sense; all men should submit their lives, their wills, and even their minds, to him. But as we shall see in our consideration of man, this is difficult and far harder than most preachers will admit. One does not acknowledge another as his lord, especially in the radical Biblical sense, unless something drastic happens to him that changes his whole understanding of his relationship to his lord. Thus, in the New Testament, Paul writes: " No one can say ' Jesus is Lord ' except by the Holy Spirit " (I Cor. 12:3).

But the term " lord " had a further meaning. A lord, if a good lord, and in the Bible God is a good Lord, not only demands and deserves absolute submission and obedience, he is also concerned for the welfare of his slaves. The slave can find his greatest joy and creativity only in complete obedience. Thus, in the Biblical sense, *the acknowledgment of God (or Christ) as Lord is not the negation of the individual but his fulfillment.* To subject even the mind and thinking to God is not to destroy the mind nor to deny the importance of reason; rather, it is to save both the mind and reason from anarchy. In any event, the Bible speaks quite properly of God as Lord and to acknowledge him seriously as Lord is a far more radical step than most people realize.

The Bible also speaks of God as *Judge.* The concept of God as Judge, while fortunately never completely lost, has become distasteful to many moderns. It became distasteful because the idea of Judge implies that there is something which needs judgment — possibly ourselves. This idea, at least in many modern circles, clashed with the popular idea that man is really not a sinner but that he is a pretty good fellow. His mistakes are due to ignorance and bad conditioning rather than to any inherent sin. He needs education, not judgment. Consequently in many circles the concept of Love supplanted the concept of Judge. As we shall see in a moment God is also Love, but these advocates of love without judgment forget that there can be no real love without judgment. The parent who does not judge and discipline his child does not truly love his child. (See Heb. 12:7-11.) Actually, as the Bible rightly understands, it is impossible to establish any basis for moral purpose or righteousness without a Judge and it is impossible to establish any basis for love, or for ethics, or justice. Right and wrong, good and bad become meaningless terms unless there is a Judge who stands above the relativities of human existence and passes judgment upon the quality of human effort. If God is not a stern and determined Judge, he is not God at all. But the Bible claims that God is such a Judge, and, in spite of sentimental appeals to Jesus as Kindly Friend and Teacher of Love (all of which have some truth in them), no one is more rigorous in his judgments than Jesus (see Matt. 23:13-36; Luke 6:24-26).

Volumes could and have been written on the theme that God is *Love*. There is no intention here to go into an elaborate discussion of this theme, for it is probably the most widely accepted designation of God there is among Christians. Perhaps it is worth pointing out, however, that no other religion reveals the love of God as does Biblical religion. But the love revealed in the Bible is not the sentimental love so often portrayed; it certainly is not divorced from judgment and punishment. It is most significant that whereas most other ancient people interpreted a national catastrophe, such as defeat in war as the failure of their gods, the Old Testament prophets interpreted national catastrophe as the judgment of God revealing his corrective love for his people. In fact, God judges and punishes only because he does love. And finally " when the time had fully come " (since man was so completely confused and involved in sin that he could not save himself) God entered the human scene and took man's frustrations and sin upon himself as a supreme act of love. The complicated question of the atonement will be discussed later, but whatever interpretation is put upon it, it stands for the conviction, *not* that the God of love considers sin of no importance requiring no judgment, but that he considers it of such importance that God himself took on the burden of the judgment. Thus, according to Biblical faith God is revealed as the Creator who judges but only because he loves.

According to the Bible, God is also designated as *Holy*. The term " holy " is difficult to define precisely, although most people have an intuitive feeling of what it means. *Webster's International Dictionary* defines it as applied to Deity, " having the character which evokes reverence and adoration, embodying spiritual perfection, free from possible defilement." All of these definitions are accurate enough, but their significance is lost unless one stops to realize that no human being is spiritually perfect and free from possible defilement and, further, that when the imperfect comes into the presence of the perfect, the only possible attitude is one of humiliation, reverence, awe, and adoration. But partly because these terms have currently lost much of their original power, they do not fully convey the meaning of holy. As Rudolf Otto has pointed out, the term "holy," religiously understood, includes an overwhelming sense of the *Mysterium Tremendum*—something so tremendous and so mysterious that man's mind cannot fully comprehend it but man is completely humbled by it. Writes Paul Tillich: "The holy is the quality of that which concerns man ultimately. . . . Only that which gives man ultimate concern has the quality of holiness."[19]

The Biblical picture of God at Mt. Sinai (Ex. 19:16-24), where God is portrayed as veiled terror ready to break out upon the people, has frequently been described by the superficial as merely a very primitive conception of God, later to be outgrown and unworthy of a so-called high religion. Nevertheless, this passage with its pictorial language has a profound truth, namely, that God is too tremendous, too mysterious, too awe-ful, for men to be familiar with. This is also something of the meaning of the term "holy"—one does not become chummy with the Ultimate! In order that the reader may have some idea of its full power, I suggest for a moment that he think seriously of how he would feel if it were known for certain that tomorrow morning at nine he would have to face God, "unto whom *all* desires are known, and from whom *no* secrets are hid." Except for the further revelation that God is love (especially as revealed in Jesus Christ) such a meeting would be too terrifying to endure. When Isaiah had his vision of the Holy God, he cried: "Woe is me! For I am lost" (Isa. 6:5). The New Testament echoes the same idea when it declares, "It is a fearful thing to fall into the hands of the living God" (Heb. 10:31). The Bible declares that God is Holy in this sense and indeed he must be if he is truly God.

4. The Providence of God

The word *Providence* as applied to God, like the word "Trinity," does not appear in the Bible. But also like the Trinity, it is implied throughout. One of the unique characteristics of the Bible is its insistence "in season and out of season" that God not only once created the world (and then let it run its course) but that he continually works at it. Not a sparrow "will fall to the ground without your Father's will" (Matt. 10: 29). All the events of history are under God's control. The events of the chosen people (Israel) are especially under the direction of God rather than being accidental, or even the results of their own efforts (Deut. 7: 7-8). Nevertheless, although the nations of the world "are like a drop from a bucket, and are accounted as the dust on the scales" (Isa. 40: 15), God has arranged the history of Israel's enemies as well as that of Israel itself (Amos, ch. 9). The call of Abraham, the exodus, the rise of the Kingdom, even its destruction and restoration, are all seen as evidences of divine Providence. And "when the time had fully come, God sent forth his Son." (Gal. 4: 4.) Certainly the New Testament Church considered that not only its creation but also its preservation and continued growth, in spite of all obstacles, could be explained only as God's providence (Acts 15: 28).

Many people turn away from Christianity because of its insistence on the providence of God, which providence they simply cannot see working out either in the world or in their own lives. In other words, they are profoundly aware of what is called the problem of evil and do not see how a good and providential God can permit such diabolical suffering as obviously goes on in the world. The final Christian answer to the problem of evil will have to wait until we have considered more fully the revelation of Jesus Christ. For the moment, however, part of the difficulty of these people arises from a misunderstanding of the Biblical meaning of providence. Unfortunately, providence in the popular mind means either having good fortune, or escaping bad fortune, both of which are defined as good or bad in terms which the individual considers good or bad. Particularly is it believed that if one is "good" and "religious," God will see to it that everything works out "all right."

There is some Biblical basis for this interpretation, especially in the Old Testament. The ancient Hebrews had no sense of a life after death and even Sheol (a relatively late conception of Hebrew thought) was a dim, dull place where both good and bad continued a drab, unenviable existence. Since God was believed to be just, if there were to be any rewards for virtue, or punishments for vice, these, of necessity, had to take place in this world. Consequently the Hebrews developed what is called the doctrine of retribution. It appears especially in Deuteronomy, Proverbs, and in some of the psalms, such as Psalm One, but it is also a major theme of their writing of history. According to this doctrine men and nations receive in this life exactly what they deserve. Health, wealth, and a long life were believed to be the results of virtue; misfortune, disease, and untimely death were prima-facie evidence of sin. It was sometimes difficult to work out the theory in practice, as in the case of the untimely death of the good king, Josiah (II Chron. 35:20-27). But it was always recognized that God "sees not as man sees" (I Sam. 16:7). Partly because it is true that in some sense life does pay us back in the same coin we put into it, and partly because people who do what they believe is right, especially if it involves same sacrifice, very much want to believe that they will be rewarded, it is not difficult to see how the idea arose that providence means getting me the food fortune that I want (and believe I deserve) and escaping the bad fortune I do not want.

Unfortunately life in this world does not work out quite that neatly. It simply is not true that the good always get health, wealth, and long life, and that the evil always get poverty, disease, and death. As a matter of fact, as far as rewards in this world are concerned, a shrewd amount of dishonesty will be more successful than strict honesty (see Luke 16:1-8). Certainly it is impossible to say today that the people of Korea or Hungary are so much more sinful than other people that they deserve the terrible destruction they have received. This thesis can be extended to every area of life and its creates an impossible problem for the conventional idea of providence. The Bible also recognizes this. The writer of Ecclesiastes challenged the whole doctrine of retribution, cynically; the writer of Job challenged it profoundly. Some of the great prophets such as Jeremiah, Ezekiel, and especially Deutero-Isaiah also challenged it. In fact, as Reinhold Niebuhr has pointed out, it was the prophets' wrestling with the problem of the justice of God in the face of the hard realities of life which drove them to find a solution in the coming of a Messiah.[20] In other words, at its more profound levels, the Old Testament recognizes that the providence of God cannot be equated with getting me the good fortune I want in this world.

The weight of the New Testament is definitely on the side that the providence of God does not necessarily mean good fortune here and now. It is true that in the teachings of Jesus there are occasional references to the righteous receiving some kind of material rewards in this world, as: "There is no man who has left house or wife or brothers or parents or children, for the sake of the kingdom of God, who will not receive manifold more in this time, and in the age to come eternal life" (Luke 18:29-30). (Mark 10:30 agrees that some of the rewards are "now in this time," but significantly adds "with persecutions." Matthew, in a parallel passage [ch. 19:27-30], says nothing about "in this time," but only, "in the new world.") However, in so far as it is safe to argue from the recorded teachings of Jesus, the weight is on the side that the providence of God should not be expected to work out in terms of material success in this world. In the Sermon on the Mount, we are admonished to love our enemies, go the second mile, give to those who ask, and so on, not because it will necessarily make the world better, or make life materially better for us, but simply in order that we may be sons of our Father who is in heaven (Matt. 5:45). No other reward is offered. We are to forgive men their trespasses against us because then "your heavenly Father also will forgive you" (Matt. 6:14). Over and over again in a variety of ways Jesus warns that becoming his disciple means taking up a cross. The rewards of discipleship are not the rewards of this world, "where moth and rust consume and where thieves break in and steal" (Matt. 6:19-20). When James and John came asking for preferred seats in the Kingdom as reward for their having followed him, Jesus promised them nothing except that they should drink "the cup that I drink" (Mark 10:35-45; Matt. 20:20-28). But it is when we turn from the teaching to the revelation in the life and work of our Lord that the popular conception of providence is most completely refuted. For the moment, putting the question of Jesus' divinity aside, still, from a strictly human point of view, if there ever was a good man it was Jesus. If the idea of providence means that the good get the good rewards in this world, Jesus should have lived a long and prosperous life, filled with the honors of men. The simple fact is that according to human standards of success he was a failure, his message was rejected, his friends deserted him, and he died a criminal, after a very brief ministry, while still a rather young man. It would be incredible, if it were not a fact, that subsequent Christians, in the light of the centrality of the cross, should distort the meaning of God's providence to mean that the good can expect good in material terms just because they are good.

Obviously then according to the Bible, at its more profound levels and especially according to the New Testament, the providence of God does not mean that the saints can expect to escape their share of life's frustrations and tragedies just because they are trying to be saints. As Bishop Aulén writes: "Faith in God's providence cannot mean that man is thereby immune from all suffering and pain. In the face of actual facts such an interpretation appears unrealistic and cannot be verified by faith itself." [21] Yet the idea of God's providence is dominant in the Bible and in Christian thought. It is seen in the whole miraculous history of Israel and in the miraculous growth and continuance of the Church (which is frequently looked upon as the continuation of the "true Israel"; see Rom., chs. 9 to 11). It is seen at the personal level in such statements as that of Paul: "We know that in everything God works for good with those who love him" (Rom. 8:28). But if God's providence does not mean material well-being, what does it mean and what is its significance for daily living?

In the first chapter I tried to make as clear as I could that Christianity is a supranatural religion. Among other things this means that, properly understood, man exists in a double situation with a reference both to this world and to the "other" world and that of the two, the "other" world is the more important. As Christians we are in the world but not of it and as Paul wrote, "Our commonwealth is in heaven" (Phil. 3:20). This otherworldly emphasis in Christianity is repugnant to many moderns; yet it is an inescapable fact of Christian faith going back to Jesus himself (see, among others, Matt. 5:11-12, 19-21; Luke 6:22-23; 10:20) and it is the Christian solution to the problem of evil as well as the mystery of providence. New Testament faith does not expect material rewards for discipleship (rather it expects persecution) but it claims, because of the work of Jesus Christ, that there is a God who, when the total situation, including the reality of the other world, is considered, will bring his faithful to victory. To quote again from Bishop Aulén, "The meaning of Christian faith in God's care is an unconditioned trust in that God is sovereign in relation to evil,"[22] or, as Paul so magnificently expressed it: "If God is for us, who is against us? . . . I am sure that neither death, nor life, nor angels, nor principalities, nor things present, nor things to come, nor powers, . . . nor anything else in all creation, will be able to separate us from the love of God in Christ Jesus our Lord" (Rom. 8:31, 38-39). It is this unconditional trust that God is sovereign even in relation to evil, and this knowledge that nothing can separate us from the love of God in Christ Jesus, which enables the Christian to accept the misfortunes of life and still work enthusiastically in the world. The Christian knows that nothing in the world can ultimately defeat him. Thus, the real meaning of providence is confidence and courage.

CHAPTER

IV

Man

1. The Ambiguous Nature of Man

In the preceding chapter, the statement was made: "religion must be of use to men or else it is of no use at all." There is no sense in holding a system of beliefs unless in some way it helps personal living. Certainly Christianity, like everything else, must demonstrate that it meets the needs of ordinary men and women involved in the process of living lives in our strenuous and difficult kind of world. Otherwise it is a waste of time. The chief reason for being a Christian is not that one thereby gets some sort of celestial fire insurance, but rather that one may have LIFE here and now.[23] "I came that they may have life, and have it abundantly." (John 10: 10.) It is the claim of Christianity that it does understand and meet the problems of human life better than anything else, but before that claim can be established it is necessary to understand the nature of man. That is a real problem.

What is man? It is fairly easy to define man in terms of some one of his aspects, and then each of the definitions will be true for that aspect, but not for a total understanding of man. Aristotle defined man as a "political animal," the anthropologists as a "toolmaking animal," the chemists as a "physiochemical being," the philosophers as a "reasoning animal," the mystics as a "spiritual being," and so forth. Each of these definitions is true as far as it goes, but none goes far enough. Man, whatever else he may be, is too complex to be understood completely in terms of any one of these definitions. If we are to understand man at all, a more comprehensive definition must be found.

As a beginning point, it is obvious that man is an animal. If he is a special kind of animal with attributes that go beyond sheer animality, these attributes cannot negate his animality. In common with all other animals, indeed with all living organisms, man must fulfill certain basic functions and is limited by these. He is limited in time and space; he must breathe, eat, drink, sleep, and eliminate; and like every other living thing, in the end he dies and returns to dust (Gen. 3:19). Man is an inevitable part of the natural order. As we have observed, that is the element of truth in all naturalistic philosophies.

This understanding of man as part of the natural order also has a sound Biblical base. Whether one takes the first Creation story (Gen., chs. 1 to 2:4a) where man and woman are created together as the last act of creation, or whether one takes the second Creation story (beginning Gen. 2:4b and following) where man is created first and woman at the end, it is clear that man is part of the created natural order. This identification is made even clearer in the second Creation story where the other animals are created before woman in order to find a suitable companion for man, and it is not until "but for the man there was not found a helper fit for him" (Gen. 2:20), that Eve is created. It is also significant that in the Biblical picture of the final consummation, man does not enter the Kingdom of God alone and independent of the natural world. All nature is included. "The wolf shall dwell with the lamb, and the leopard shall lie down with the kid, and the calf and the lion and the fatling together, and a little child shall lead them. . . . For the earth shall be full of the knowledge of the Lord" (Isa. 11:6, 9). And Paul writes to the Romans, "For the creation waits with eager longing for the revealing of the sons of God, . . . because the creation itself will be set free from its bondage to decay and obtain the glorious liberty of the children of God" (Rom. 8:19, 21). Thus, the Bible makes as explicit as any naturalistic philosophy that man is a creature bound by the conditions of creatureliness and a part of the natural order. (In so far as mysticism attempts to deny, negate, or escape from the basic given of man's involvement in the natural world it is un-Biblical.) In fact, if anything, the Biblical position goes beyond the naturalistic position in this regard, for, as we shall see later, it declares that when man forgets that he is part of creation, subject to his Creator, and tries to act as though this were not so, he sins.

The beginning point, then, for all thinking about man is that he is inexorably a part of the natural created world. To make such a statement is not to sell hostages to the naturalist; it is to recognize a fact that has a sound Biblical basis. But the Bible, for all its emphasis on man as a creature and a part of the created order, also declares that man is a special creature, created " in the image of God " (Gen. 1:27), which simply means that man has been created for a special relationship with God and that he has capacities, usually referred to as " spiritual capacities," for responding to that relationship. In fact, Biblical religion insists that only when man responds fully to that relationship does he reach his full capacities of creative manhood.

In the light of modern science, and particularly of some of modern psychology, is this Biblical claim for the nature of man justifiable? Are these so-called " spiritual capacities " completely explainable within a framework of glands, and chemistry, and phenomena which are all reducible to purely natural processes; or do they actually point to an order of human existence which cannot be reduced to the strictly natural? In the last analysis, I suppose, the answer given will rest, as we saw in the first chapter, on assumptions of faith; but Christians believe that there are certain demonstrable facts of human nature and experience which indicate that man cannot be completely reduced to natural phenomena and which point to a kinship with another order of reality. I suggest certain evidences to support this position.

The first evidence is found in the *universal sense of " oughtness " or " duty "* which we have discussed in the preceding chapter in connection with the arguments for belief in God. Beyond what was said there, it is of considerable significance that our sense of oughtness frequently drives us to do certain things that necessitate sacrificing our purely natural interests. Depending on time, place, and circumstance, a man may feel that he ought to be forgiving to his enemies, or he may feel that he ought to take revenge upon his enemies. In either case, in one way or another, it may involve him in actions and consequences that hurt his family, or himself, or his interests and well-being as a purely natural man. Thus, the sense of oughtness, however it may be derived, is not only universal, it can lead men to do that which is " unnatural."

A little later we shall consider the question of freedom versus determinism, but at the moment it is worth pointing out that even those who claim to be complete determinists cannot escape this sense of oughtness. Regardless of what they may claim to believe in theory, in actual practice all men feel on certain occasions, if not actual qualms of conscience, at least qualms that they should have done differently. No matter how much a man may try to tell himself that he is the victim of circumstance and conditioning, and that he is not responsible for his decisions, all men, at least on certain occasions, do feel responsible for their decisions —particularly when they turn out badly. It is absurd to have a sense of responsibility for one's decisions if one is a purely natural being, for a purely natural being ought only to act naturally and have no regrets and no sense of conscience. The fact that all men, at some points, do have a sense of responsibility for their actions points to an element in the human personality which lifts man above the purely natural.

The capacity to go beyond. Another universal characteristic of man is his ability to " go beyond " or " step outside " of any given situation in which he is and to imagine himself in a different situation. This ability is most simply illustrated in our capacity for daydreaming. In our daydreams we can step outside of, or go beyond, the real situation in which we live and in imagination live in another situation. We can recall the past and relive a situation that no longer exists; we can anticipate the future and cast ourselves in heroic roles that have only a remote connection with reality. More important, we can dream of a future that does not now exist, and at least to some degree we can change both ourselves and the world to approximate the vision of that dream. Indeed, it is this human capacity to go beyond the immediate situation and dream of a different situation which makes possible all the creative works of man. That this human characteristic to dream is dangerous goes without saying. It is possible to dream of a world so different from the real world and to live so in terms of that imagined world that the dreamer goes insane. Nevertheless, the fact that this power is abused and that people do go insane is, in itself, an evidence of the human capacity to "go beyond."

Another aspect of this capacity to "go beyond" is man's ability to pass judgment on himself. This is related to the previous point about "oughtness." It is possible to have a sense of oughtness only because in some way or other it is possible to get outside oneself and criticize oneself from some other point of view. Everyone, from time to time, has had the experience of feeling that he has become disassociated from himself and that he is watching himself as a spectator watches a play. Then he passes judgment on himself. Perhaps the most extreme illustration of this is suicide. In suicide it is possible for a man to get so completely outside himself that he can declare his own existence intolerable and end it. Why is this possible? The most reasonable explanation seems to be that there is in man, whether it be called the spirit, or the soul, or the mind, or what not — a something which cannot be limited to the purely natural. If we were completely and totally limited to our natural selves, we would have no basis for judgment or criticism of ourselves. Such a judgment and criticism automatically presupposes another perspective. The capacity for judgment, of necessity, requires a certain separation from what is judged. To illustrate by analogy:[24] If everything in the world were blue, we should have no consciousness of the color blue. In fact we should have no consciousness of any color at all; blue would simply be standard without our ever realizing its color. Blueness becomes blue only because we are aware of some other color, not blue, in terms of which blueness is judged and recognized as blue. Thus, this strange human phenomenon of being able to get outside of oneself, to go beyond the realities of a particular given situation, and to change the situation more or less in terms of what does not exist but is only imagined, necessarily presupposes that there is that in man which makes him more than just a natural animal.

The sense of dread. Man's capacity for dread is a profound fact of human nature which has only recently received serious attention as a result of the development of psychology, psychoanalysis, and psychotherapy. Had we been more discerning we would have realized that the Bible understood and spoke of this element of dread in various places, such as in the story of the Fall, Gideon's desire for certainty, the soul struggles of the prophets, notably Jeremiah, and also in Job and some of the psalms, to mention only a few Old Testament instances. In the New Testament the stories of the demonic possession and Jesus' cure of it, as well as the preaching of the apostles about sin and forgiveness are pregnant in this regard. In modern times and religiously speaking, it was Sören Kierkegaard who called us back to the significance of the concept of dread.

The concept of dread is difficult to define precisely. Kierkegaard uses the term *Angst,* for which there is no exact English translation. The words " dread " and " anxiety " are usually used. *Angst,* or dread, or anxiety, includes fear, but it goes farther than the usual meaning of fear. Normally we think of fear as fear of something specific and known. We are afraid of something in particular concerning which we know something — pain, failure, or death. When the occasion of the fear is over, fear subsides and we return to normal. In this sense fear is fear of what is known. *Angst,* on the other hand, is a more deep-seated fear or anxiety of what is unknown. It is a dread of nothingness and meaninglessness. For instance, one of the dominating, perhaps *the* most dominating, questions asked by each of us (often subconsciously), and one that controls most of our lives, is: " What is going to happen to me? " Each of us, if we are honest and think about it, will admit that we ask this question over and over again, " in season and out." Most of what we do is done to try to make the answer to that question come out as satisfactorily to us as possible. But the question never can completely and permanently be answered to our satisfaction, partly because our desires are virtually limitless and partly because, consciously or unconsciously, each of us knows that he stands under the threat of forces over which he has no control, and ultimately under the threat of death.

Why does this question, that of " What is going to happen to me? " arise and haunt us so persistently? It arises because when all is said and done we have an unconquerable feeling that we are alone in an alien world. (The psychological basis for this will be given shortly.) This feeling of aloneness is expressed in another feeling, common to each of us, " Nobody really understands me." We sometimes say our wives know us better than we know ourselves. In one sense probably they do. In another sense, more profound, not even our wives or our most intimate friends understand us as we understand ourselves. We feel that we are alone in an alien world and this appears to us a dreadful situation, so dreadful that most of the time we do not want to think about it. But we cannot escape it. This is something of what is meant by *Angst* or dread, or anxiety.

I do not know much about subhuman animal psychology. Perhaps my dog has some sense of *Angst* too, but from my observation he does not appear to. He fears specific things and situations but he does not appear to be anxious about an unknown future. Be that as it may, man, at least, knows not only animal fear of the known, but he also knows what might be called a deeper spiritual fear, a dread of what is unknown. Especially he dreads and is anxious about the possibility of nothingness and meaninglessness. In this concept of dread which is universally characteristic of every person we have evidence that man is not completely a part of the natural world. If the word " natural " means anything at all, it is a contradiction in terms for the strictly natural to dread and be anxious about what is strictly natural. The concept of dread points to the fact that man is somewhat in conflict with his natural world and therefore is a being related to another order of existence.

If this analysis is correct, it is obvious that man's nature is too complex to be understood in terms of any one category. The real job is to explain man's nature in a way that does justice to all the facts. On the way to doing this let me first summarize.

On the one hand man is clearly a part of nature. He is a part of and a creature of the natural world and (in this life) he cannot escape this fact. This means that what man can do is limited to certain natural conditions which he must fulfill and which he shares with the rest of natural life. Man is limited by time and space and in the end he dies. "You are dust, and to dust you shall return." (Gen. 3: 19.) The same is true of animal and plant life. All of this means that man is a creature, part of the created order and limited by the conditions of his creatureliness. Further, in so far as a man continues to live, he is under the necessity of making decisions and of acting on them; these decisions and actions place further limitations upon him. On the one hand, then, man is a creature, finite and limited.

On the other hand, man is something more than a mere creature. He has a conscience which passes judgment on himself and on events. He hopes and he dreads. He can step outside himself and go beyond any given situation and in some measure change both himself and the situation to fulfill partially his hopes or to forestall his fears. Man can get so completely outside himself that he can deny both himself and his world, either in an act of self-sacrifice or in an act of self-destruction. Man is a creator as well as a creature. He does create new situations and new ways of dealing with old situations. In any creation there are always virtually an infinite number of possibilities. These always fall within limits but they are still virtually infinite. For instance, a poet being asked to write a sonnet on a sunset is limited by his subject and by the sonnet form, but he has an infinite choice of words and arrangement. Thus man is a creature with infinite possibilities for creativeness.

On this basis the old question of freedom versus determinism becomes largely meaningless. To say that man is either free or determined is nonsense. It is not a matter of being "either/or"; it is rather a question of being " both/and." Man is neither completely free nor completely determined. He is free for infinite possibilities within a framework of limitation. Paradoxically he is most free to be creative when he best understands his limitations. The whole conclusion might be stated in the following proposition:

Man's fundamental nature is too complex to be understood in simple terms of any one category whether it be that of the physical scientist, the social scientist, the naturalistic psychologist, the philosopher, or the mystic. Man's nature can be understood only in paradoxical terms. He is both a part of the natural order and of an order beyond nature at the same time, both free and determined at the same time, both finite and infinite at the same time; and within the structures of finiteness he can participate in infinite creativity.

2. The Origin and Meaning of Self-consciousness

It is now time to turn to the explanation of the basis of this paradoxical nature of man.

Whatever else we may be aware of, each of us is aware of himself. A man may not understand all about himself and he may not always understand why he does some of the things he does. I believe it is a psychological axiom that no one can psychoanalyze himself completely and accurately. Nevertheless each of us is conscious of himself as being a definite Self. Whatever else he may or may not know, in so far as it is possible to say that man knows anything at all, he knows that he is an existing Self.

There is a famous story of René Descartes: One winter day he climbed into an oven and tried to discover what it was possible to doubt as existing and what it was impossible to doubt as existing. After long concentration Descartes came to the conclusion that he could doubt the existence of everything and everybody, but that he could not doubt that he was doing the doubting. As a result of this effort he made his famous dictum, " *Cogito, ergo sum* " — " I think, therefore I am." For my part, I am not sure that " I think " is the most basic fact; I suspect that " I feel," or " I am aware," would be more accurate. At any rate, Descartes was pointing to something in every human being which exists beyond doubt although it cannot be called a thing in a material sense. Descartes established the reality of the Self and it is significant that he had to establish it before he could establish the reality of anything else; for everything else in the world is known only as it is known by existing Selves. Now, what is a Self? What does it mean to be a Self? How does a Self become conscious of itself and what makes this knowledge possible?

As we have seen above, man is a paradoxical being who, on the one hand, is a part of his world and, on the other hand, is at the same time independent of (can go beyond) his world. How do I know that I am to some extent independent of my world? I know it because I am at least partly opposed to, and in conflict with, the rest of the world. Whatever else I know, I know that I am not you, reader, nor my wife, nor my friend. I know that I am not this desk on which I write, and I am not the chair in the corner. I know this because although all things and people may be of help and even of necessity to me in my voyage through life, they (both things and people) are also at times obstacles which provide opposition for me and which have to be circumvented. In some sense I know that I am completely other than and in opposition to everything and everybody. Such knowledge is only possible if, also in some sense, I am separated from them, independent of them, and therefore an independent and separated Self. The illustration of blueness given above is applicable here too. The very fact that I know that I am not my friend, nor that chair, that I know that I am other than and opposed to my world, can be explained only by presupposing a certain degree of independence. Therefore, self-consciousness arises partly from the fact that I am aware of a world to which I am opposed.

That is one half of the business. The other half is that, as we have also seen above, I am very much a part of my world. I belong to the world; I am in it and I need it. It is only because there is a world to which I belong that I have any consciousness of being opposed to it or other than it. Presuming the impossible for the sake of an illustration: If a baby could be born and reared in a complete vacuum, it would never develop self-consciousness. It is only because I meet people, bump into tables, sit on chairs, and so forth, that I am aware of a world that is not I. In other words, it is only my inevitable involvement in the world which makes it possible for me to be conscious of myself as independent of and separated from the world. To put the matter in propositional form: *The basis of self-consciousness rests on man's fundamental situation in existence as that of being a definite Self only because he has a world to which he both belongs and is opposed at the same time.*

If this is true, there are some very important implications. First of all, this means that each person is an individual. I am not my friend and my friend is not I; each of us is unique—separate and other than everything else and everybody else. This is the fundamental basis of all demands, philosophical, religious, and political, for individualism; each person must be treated as an individual. Any system of philosophy, or of government, or even of ecclesiastical organization, which tries permanently and systematically to destroy the uniqueness of the individual tries to destroy what is basically inherent in man; and since to deny what is basically inherent is impossible, such a system will eventually destroy itself.

Each of us, then, is a unique individual experiencing life each in his unique way. But this fact of the uniqueness of our individualism has a further implication which is not altogether pleasant, for to be really an individual is to be alone. In some very real sense each of us is an isolated Self, a Self in solitude. This is why we never completely escape the feeling, "Nobody understands me." Not only does no one really understand me, but also no one really can save me, nor can I save anyone else. Each person is a separate individual who alone can make his own decisions. One person may advise another and the advice may be of help, but no one can really decide for another ("Work out your own salvation with fear and trembling," Phil. 2:12). Anyone who tries to decide for another treats him as less than a person and assumes prerogatives that belong only to God, thereby committing blasphemy. This is why Kierkegaard in *Purity of Heart* and Bunyan in *The Pilgrim's Progress* quite rightly, although in different ways, admonish the reader that even wife, or husband, or family (the closest human fellowships there are) cannot save him, and that if these stand in the way of his salvation it is better to break with them. And our Lord said: " If any one comes to me and does not hate his own father and mother and wife and children and brothers and sisters, yes, and even his own life, he cannot be my disciple." (Luke 14:26.)

The fact that man is an individual means that man is, in the last analysis, utterly alone. This situation of aloneness is not merely unpleasant; it is actually terrifying. To be really and completely alone is perhaps the most terrible thing that can happen to a person. (It is the exploitation of this fact that enables the communists to break the strongest personalities to the point where they will deny their entire life training.) Obviously by being alone I do not mean just being by oneself for a while; most intelligent people want a certain amount of privacy, although the fact that so few people like to be alone for any length of time is indicative. I mean, rather, the deeper sense of aloneness which one may have even in the midst of a crowd. Actually we may be more conscious of being alone when we are in a crowd than when we are by ourselves, for the crowd reminds us of our separateness. I mean the sense of aloneness that is expressed in the phrase, " Nobody understands me." This is terrifying and it can drive people to all kinds of desperate action including insanity and suicide.

Incidentally, it is here that we discover the true cause of the fear of death (*Angst*). It is not that death may be painful. It is rather that at death we must give up all that is familiar and all that gives most people whatever security they have; we must face an unknown future alone. All our lives long we manage to make fairly successful attempts to escape facing the full significance of our individuality, but at death all our escape devices break down. Each of us must die his own death; no one else can do it for us. Death is first of all an isolating experience that reveals to us how completely we are alone. This is terrifying, and this is why most people fear death. The power of *Angst* arises not only from fear of the unknown but from the fact that we must face the unknown alone.

This situation, that of aloneness, is intolerable. But we are not merely Selves in isolation; we are Selves who are aware of our isolation because we are also part of a world to which we belong. It is this second fact of human experience, namely, the fact that we do belong to and are a part of the world, which makes life tolerable for most people. Because of our relationship to the world we can go out and create at least temporary [25] forms of community which help us to overcome our aloneness. Indeed, it is the desire to overcome our aloneness, coupled with the fact that we are a part of the world, which is the source of all man's creative activities. Because we cannot tolerate our aloneness we go out and make friends, build communities, form clubs and groups, and try to establish neighborly and brotherhood relationships. In fact, when one thinks about it, we spend most of our time doing the things we do in order to establish relationships with others and to gain the approval and recognition of others, and so to overcome our sense of aloneness. Thus, it is the fact of man's situation as being a Self who knows he is alone because he is opposed to a world to which he belongs, which is at the same time the basis not only of individualism but also of community. It provides the basic drive for all man's social creative efforts.

The more recent developments of the "depth" or "we" psychology have thrown considerable light on this situation. The baby, when still in the mother and presumably for some time after birth, lives in an "original-we" of dependence on its mother in which it finds security. But this security of the "original-we" is only temporary. Eventually and inevitably the mother, often unintentionally and unconsciously, does something, or fails to do something (actually not once but many times), that makes the baby aware that the mother is not completely dependable. The "original-we" and its security are broken and the baby begins to be conscious of itself as being alone in an alien world. The rest of life and the process of growing up is a matter of adjusting to this situation of aloneness and of trying to find new more mature we-relationships because we are Selves in isolation, and we cannot stand it; and we can establish at least temporary and reasonably successful we-relationships because we are part of a world along with everybody else.

This analysis of human nature should make more relevant some of the claims of supranaturalism and especially of Christianity. Earlier we said that the only really good reason for being a Christian is that the Christian faith answers the problems of everyday living. Here is one of the places where Christianity does become relevant to existential living.

As should now be obvious, all men need to have a we-relationship. Without it, life becomes intolerable, indeed, impossible in any human sense. We are so constructed by the givens in human nature that we have to belong to we-groups. But all the we-relationships which are possible in this world are temporary; eventually all break up, at least as far as the individual is concerned. Even the family, which is the most powerful we-group, is broken by death if not before. If this life and this world, with the temporary we-groups that are possible within it, is all there is, then man is indeed in a diabolical situation, for the demands of the given in man's nature require a permanent " we " if man is to achieve true maturity, and no permanent " we " is possible at the human level of this natural world. In this case it follows that by some horrible combination of accidents a blind and meaningless universe has thrown up beings who, pathetically, are forever doomed to frustration. The only alternative to this tragic conclusion is the possibility of a we-relationship which can transcend this world and can overcome and negate the apparent ultimate isolation of death. It is the claim of Christianity that there is a God with whom man can establish a permanent and eternal " we," which alone gives true security and the possibility of a true and permanent maturity. Indeed, looked at rightly through the eyes of faith, Christianity declares that God seeks us before we seek him. It believes that God in his infinite wisdom and mercy has created man purposely as he is; that is, God has created man so that he will be alone and driven by his aloneness to seek we-relationships, and that the only true and permanent we-relationship can be found in God. This is what is back of Saint Augustine's famous prayer: "Thou hast made us for thyself and our souls are restless until they rest in thee." Thus Christianity offers a practical solution to one of the most basic problems of human daily living.

3. Original Sin

The understanding of man's fundamental nature as a Self in an intolerable isolation which he tries to overcome also illuminates the Christian doctrine of original sin. Unfortunately there is considerable confusion in the minds of many people today about what Christianity means by sin. Partly because of the ecclesiastical legalism of the Roman Catholic Church, and partly because of the moralistic legalism of much of Protestantism, the average man tends to think of "sins" (in the plural) and usually in terms of the moralities: drinking, swearing, stealing, adultery, lying, murder, and so forth. Emphatically these are not sins in the Christian sense, although they may be, and usually are, external expressions of the deeper sin. The fundamental sin according to the Bible is pride, egocentricity, self-deification, and the insistence that each of us is the final arbiter of what is good for him, an insistence that reveals a lack of trust in and submission to God. It is evidenced in the fact that, in seeking an answer to the perennial question, "What is going to happen to me?", we seek the good in terms which we, in the privacy of our own selfish judgment, have decided to be good. If I steal from a man, it is because I have decided in the privacy of my own judgment that my interests are more important than his interests. To make such a judgment is to assume, blasphemously, the divine right to judge between him and me. God alone has that right; for me to assume it is either actually to deny God, or to deny his goodness and trustworthiness. Thus sin is a form of self-deification.

This theme runs all through the Bible from beginning to end, but it is most explicitly stated in the second Creation story. In this story Adam and Eve are condemned not because they stole some fruit and ate an apple. The temptation of the serpent was: "You will not die. For God knows that when you eat of it your eyes will be opened, and *you will be like God,* knowing good and evil." (Gen. 3:4, 5.) The temptation to which Adam and Eve succumbed was the temptation to a pride and a self-deification which refuses to submit to God. It is a revolt of the creature against the Creator. Such a revolt cannot be successful in the long run if God is God; it is blasphemy which must be punished. And the punishment that followed, according to the story, is that Adam and Eve were driven from Paradise where they had an "original-we" relationship and security with both God and all the rest of the created order. Now they have to struggle to live in opposition to the world. It is highly significant that it was not until Adam and Eve had eaten of the fruit, that is, had defied God, that "they knew that they were naked; and . . . hid themselves" (Gen. 3:7, 8). In other words the "original-we" was broken and they became conscious of themselves as individuals and of their aloneness.

The Biblical understanding of man as revealed in the story of the Fall fits the analysis of man we have already made. As we have seen, man is a Self, conscious of himself, because he belongs to a world to which he is opposed at the same time and, therefore, he is in an intolerable state of aloneness which he tries to overcome by establishing we-relationships. But because of man's given situation there are, in every we-relationship that man tries to establish, elements of self-concern, of selfishness, and of self-assertive pride. At the heart of every altruistic and community-creating act there is a corrupting seed of selfishness and will-to-power. To admit this is not to deny the importance of altruistic and community-creating acts; if it were not for them, life would be intolerable. To love our neighbor as ourselves is the second commandment and the fact that we can satisfy our own self-concern only by community-creating (neighbor-loving) acts is seen, with the eyes of faith, as part of God's grace making human life possible. Nevertheless, in every act of community and brotherhood there is a selfish motive. It is revealed in all areas of life. It is obvious in the bully or the dictator, whether he is in government, or in the shop, or in the home. It is equally the motive of the Uriah Heep and the clinging vine who cultivate their weakness in order to get protection. It appears in the family and in all love-relationships. In his book *Sexual Tensions in Marriage,* Th. van de Velt points out that in every healthy home there is a continual war for domination, which, if completely won by one party, will cause a breakup of the home because the winner loses respect for the loser, and the loser loses respect for himself or herself. It appears even in religion. At the highest religious level it involves self-sacrifice in order to win the approval of God (which is legitimate). At lower levels it involves performing specified acts of ritual, or doing works in order to try to manipulate God to fulfill our selfish desires (which is both illegitimate and impossible). None of us ever completely escapes this element of self-concern and will-to-power, for it arises from the givens in human nature. It is what is meant by original sin.

Original sin is *original* not because long ago one historical man and woman, Adam and Eve, the historical original parents of all subsequent mankind, first committed a sin and then, by a process of biological inheritance, passed it on to their descendants forever. Such a conception makes God a fiend. Rather, it is that Adam and Eve are the prototypes of all men and women, symbolically describing the eternal human situation. We all go through the Adam and Eve experience of breaking the innocence and security of the "original-we" and of becoming self-conscious by discovering we are Selves belonging to a world to which we are opposed at the same time. And the first act in that discovery is the Adam and Eve act of self-assertion. Original sin is original because it arises from an original given nature without which man would not be man.

4. Man's Resistance

The realization that every effort to establish we-relationships arises from our self-concern and therefore involves sin illuminates other aspects of human conduct and human nature, both regarding our fellow men and regarding our attitude toward God.

Each of us needs we-groups, but because of our selfishness we also resist them. At least we tend to accept them, so far as is possible, only on our own terms. The baby enters an "original-we" which he almost completely controls. At first everything possible is done to satisfy his needs and desires. But soon, as we have seen, the mother, because of the demands of life, fails to satisfy all the baby's wants. The major part of growing up is learning to adjust and to accept the fact that we cannot always make life, or other people, submit to our desires. Consequently, for our own self-interest we try to adjust to the requirements of life as much as is necessary, *but no more than we have to.* And we all tend to join those we-groups which either offer us a maximum of what we want, or which we think can be manipulated to give us a maximum of what we want.

But in order to achieve any kind of we-relationship it is always necessary to give up something of ourselves. And the more mature and lasting the "we" the more we are required to give up. A real "we" does not exist where one person forces another to accept his terms. To be a real "we" there must always be a real giving and a real submission. But to give up ourselves is the last thing in the world any of us naturally wants to do, for it involves a kind of suicide. Consequently we resist giving up ourselves as much as we can; we seek to enter we-relationships which will preserve as much of our individuality as possible, or else we try to shape them by subtle or not so subtle means to our desires. (This is why the ideal of universal brotherhood so widely advocated by idealists is so difficult, if not impossible. These idealists forget, or have never learned, that in every attempt at brotherhood there is an element of self-concern which seeks to manipulate the group. We-groups exist because they represent a compound of the self-interests of the individuals in them and, as Reinhold Niebuhr has pointed out, the larger the group the more selfishly it inevitably acts.)

Actually most of us are caught on the horns of a dilemma. Each of us wants and needs the security of a we-group, but because becoming a real part of every such group demands that we give up something of ourselves we resist it. To a large degree we all fear and resist the thing we want. If Oscar Wilde's famous line, "Yet each man kills the thing he loves," is an overstatement, it at least points to a partial truth; for everything we love demands a sacrifice upon our part. This appears at even mundane levels. Appointment to some committee or organization offers opportunity for recognition which we want, but it also may make demands upon our time and energy more than we want. This strange ambiguous human characteristic of wanting and resisting the same thing has been analyzed by Sören Kierkegaard better than by anyone I know when, in his *The Concept of Dread,* he speaks of "sympathetic-antipathy and antipathetic-sympathy."[26] We are in fact both repelled and attracted at the same time, by the same thing, activity, and person. A new opportunity, particularly if it involves quite a change for us, may be very appealing, but at the same time it can frighten us. It is because of this ambiguity that the lives of many people consist of moving from one frustrating indecision to the next.

This situation of symapthetic-antipathy and antipathetic-sympathy, of wanting and not wanting the same thing at the same time, extends even and especially to our attitude toward God. In fact, it becomes most critical in our attitude toward God because God demands our most complete submission. Wrote the author of The Letter to the Hebrews: "It is a fearful thing to fall into the hands of the living God." (Heb. 10:31.) It certainly is! And most preachers and religious leaders in urging people to be religious have not understood how fearful it is. It is fearful because God demands that I give up far more of myself than does any human group; indeed, God demands all; and all is more than most of us are ready to give up. Consequently we resist the God we both want and need. Among the so-called irreligious and atheists, this resistance is overt. With many of these irreligious their resistance to religion is born of a conscious, or unconscious, realization that many pious religious people talk too easily about God, and that if one really accepts God, it must mean a more radical change in their lives, a more radical giving up, than they are ready to make. This is the source of a great deal of so-called atheism. It is not that the individual does not believe that there is a God; rather, it is that the individual does believe there is a God but understands that the price tag on that belief is a lot higher than the pious will admit. At least in several cases of my own counseling with self-styled atheists, each finally admitted that he (or she) really did believe in God but knew that to affirm that belief seriously would require giving up things in his or her life that could not easily be given up. To say he believed in God and to keep his current pattern of life would result in split personality (schizophrenia). Since he would not change, peace of mind could come only by denying there is a God. It should be noted that these atheists are more aware of the truth of " It is a fearful thing to fall into the hands of the living God " than are the pious, and that thus they are, in a very real sense, more honest and more religious than many of the self-styled religious.

But even those of us who try to take our faith seriously and not merely conventionally are more or less aware of our resistance to God. The simple and pathetic fact is that most of us want God, *but not too much!* We want the comforting assurance of a God somewhere in the background who can be called upon as needed, but we do not want a God who interferes with our plans and who makes demands upon us. We want a kind of supermagician who will help us to get what we cannot get for ourselves, but we do not want a God who says precisely to us, " Thou shalt! " and " Thou shalt not! " But the God who is really God is not first (in our experience) a God who comforts. He is first a God " unto whom all hearts are open, all desires known, and from whom no secrets are hid " (a terrifying thought!), who judges and commands. Consequently we all resist the God we want and need. Writes Paul Tillich: " It is safe to say that a man who has never tried to flee God has never experienced the God who is really God. . . . Man tries to escape God and hates Him. . . . The protest against God, the will that there be no God, the flight to atheism are all genuine elements of a profound religion." [27]

Recently I received a letter from a former student who took his religion with something more than conventional seriousness. After things had gone rather smoothly for some time, a serious setback in his plans occurred. "For about two weeks," he wrote me, "I was no good to myself or to the school. It upset me more than I have been upset in years and my relationship with God was shattered. For the first time in my life I resented God very much. I began to wonder . . . just how much of an autocrat God is. . . . It's awful to admit, but I actually hated him." Even, indeed especially, those who take their religion seriously are aware of their resentment of and revolt against God. They know "it *is* a fearful thing to fall into the hands of the living God." Only the superficial to whom the Christian faith is primarily a form of intellectual assent, or a form of community respectability, escape it, and they escape only as long as they continue the frustrating mediocrity of their pathetic living.

All this conscious and subconscious resentment of and revolt against God is what Christianity means by sin, for God is our maker and we belong to him. Sin is obviously far more profound than simply breaking moral rules. And no one completely escapes this situation, for its roots are in the fundamental givens of human nature: that man is a Self who is aware of himself because he belongs to a world to which he is opposed at the same time. It is original sin because it is an original part of every man's fundamental nature. Thus man, in his existential situation, is irrevocably caught in a fundamental contradiction. Man needs, wants, and strives for we-relationships and at the same time he fears and resists them and injects into those he accepts his own corrupting selfishness. This applies not only to all human we-relationships; it applies also to his relationship toward God, for all men tend either to flee from God or to try by elaborate devices (frequently ecclesiastically approved) to control God for their own interests.

If this analysis is anywhere nearly correct, then man is a sinner and in a much more serious situation than most people care to face (although fortunately in recent years there has been far more recognition of it). If there is a God at all in the Biblical sense, it then becomes axiomatic that all men ought to submit absolutely to that God and to try to do his will as best they can. But none of us submits absolutely; we are all more or less in revolt at one point or another. Therefore, it is inevitable that God comes to us first as a judge to be feared. A poor analogy would be that of going to work for a company and saying, "I do not care whether or not there is a president or what his orders are; I am going to do as I please." Just as the president of a company cannot tolerate such a procedure, neither can God.

Further, if the point of view here maintained is correct, the solution of this dilemma cannot come from any human devising, for every human being is caught in the same fundamental contradiction. Every purely human solution has in it the seeds of revolt and of its own corruption. (This is a fact for which the naturalists have no solution.) The only possible solution is one that comes from something outside of, and is not involved in, the fundamental contradiction. Every effort made by a man caught in quicksand to extricate himself only gets him in that much deeper. His only hope is to get a hold on something, to get help from someone, who is outside of, and not involved in, the quicksand. In other words the only solution is a redemption offered to man from what is outside man and yet reaches down and finds man where he is in the quicksand. Christianity and Christianity alone claims that God not only judges, as he must, but that he so loves us that he reaches down and offers that redemption in Jesus who is the Christ and both man and God. Since the redeeming role and the work of Jesus Christ are central to the Christian faith, we turn to them next.

CHAPTER

V

Jesus, Who Is the Christ

THE UNIQUE THING ABOUT CHRISTIANITY — THE THING THAT DISTINguishes it uncompromisingly from all other religions and all other philosophies — is its faith that an obscure Jewish rabbi, Jesus of Nazareth, was the Christ. The word "Christ" is not the second name of a person whose first name was Jesus; it is a title. As Paul Tillich has been insisting, strictly speaking we should not say, "Jesus Christ," but, "Jesus, the Christ," or "Jesus, who is the Christ." "Christ" is an Anglicized form of the Greek *Christos* and Latin *Christus,* which, in turn, are translations of the Hebrew word *Messiah*. The "Messiah" literally is "the anointed one"; actually it meant one who was to be especially and uniquely sent from God to redeem men from their sin, establish justice, and solve the humanly insolvable problems of human existence. In other words the Christ is one especially sent by God, God's unique revealer and incarnation bringing men new possibilities and new life.

We have discussed Jesus Christ as the Second Person of the Trinity in Chapter III. There the discussion was limited to its place in the Trinitarian formula of our understanding of God's total revelation. Now it is time to consider why Christian faith insists that Jesus of Nazareth was and is the Christ, and then what is the significance of that assertion.

1. Historical Considerations

First of all, I would remind the reader of a very important theoretical point regarding not only Christian faith but all historical data. The ideal of historians of a generation or so ago, that they should gather only objective facts free from all interpretations and then let the facts speak for themselves, is now recognized as impossible. It is now generally recognized that in dealing with historical data, and this becomes especially true with the data of ancient history, we always deal with both facts and interpretations inseparably mixed together. The only facts we can get in history are facts recorded by men who, consciously or unconsciously, held a philosophy or world-view which inevitably colored their recording of the facts. Further, a fact by itself (if that were possible) is meaningless until some interpretation has been attached to it. Contrariwise, to be historically valid, there must be a historical fact to which the interpretation refers — otherwise the interpretation is not an interpretation of a fact but an illusion. Interpreted facts are the most that historical science can recover. This is a limitation of all historical research and it applies to every historical person as much as to Jesus of Nazareth. The New Testament is essentially the interpretation of the significance of Jesus of Nazareth. Actually it is several interpretations, for each writer has his own, but all of them point to the same person, and in spite of differences, all assert he was the Christ.

There must, however, be the historical fact — otherwise, as we have seen, the interpretations are not interpretations of fact but only imaginative illusions, or delusions. It is at this point that we run into the first difficulty, for the facts of the life of Jesus are far more obscure than was once thought. In the late nineteenth and early twentieth centuries, Christian scholars, baffled by the confusion of theories about Christ and under attacks from science and the cult of historical objectivity, sought a solution in the attempt to " discover the historical Jesus." If we could only get behind the " Christ of faith " to the facts of the life and teachings of Jesus, it was asserted, they would be discovered to be sufficiently attractive to win men's allegiance. It would also be reasonable and intellectually respectable.[28] Great effort, scholarship, and devotion were put into this enterprise and much was discovered. Ironically, however, what was discovered was not what was hoped for or expected. The more scholars delved into the records the vaguer the historical Jesus became. The further they went, the more they discovered that there was less and less historical objective data free from interpretations.

It must be remembered that Jesus himself left no written documents. The only record of his writing at all is the out-of-context story of the woman taken in adultery when "Jesus bent down and wrote with his finger on the ground" (John 8:6). The only existent records of his life and teaching are found in the four Gospels and these were written a generation or more after the events recorded in an age that did not use stenographic reports or dictaphones.[29] We do not know exactly when Jesus was born except that it was probably not on December 25. Scholars usually say he was born between 6 and 4 B.C. but, depending on which Gospel text you use, the date can be anywhere between 15 B.C. and A.D. 9. We do not know when he died, except that it was during the proconsulship of Pontius Pilate (A.D. 26–36). We do not know how long his ministry lasted. (The Synoptic Gospels—Matthew, Mark, and Luke—imply one year or less; John's Gospel implies three years.) Strictly speaking, in a scientific sense we cannot be absolutely certain that we have any one of his teachings as he gave it. It is now generally recognized that each of the Gospels not only was written about thirty or more years after his death but also was written by men who held the faith that Jesus was the Christ and who were trying to convince others to accept that faith. In other words each of the Gospels represents the belief of the Early Church about the significance of Jesus in the time and place in which it was written. Therefore the attempt to bypass "the Christ of faith" and to discover "the historical Jesus" has ended in the realization that the Jesus of history can be recovered only through the faith of the Early Church, and that the Early Church was only interested in Jesus because it was convinced that he was the Christ.

So sweeping are the results of this historical research that it is leading some scholars to abandon the whole attempt to rediscover the historical Jesus. Writes Robert C. Johnson in an illuminating article on this whole problem: [30]

"Today this [back to the historical Jesus] movement is dead. A 'life of Jesus' is an anachronism. And not only is the movement dead, but in somewhat characteristic fashion the pendulum of theology has tended to make a complete arc and come to rest on the other extreme. Now we are variously told that 'it is not the least needful for salvation to know Christ according to the flesh' (Santayana); that 'the foundation of Christian belief is not the historical Jesus, an unknown historical personality' (Tillich); that the meager information about him as can be culled proves to be 'unilluminating.' . . ."

The question immediately rises whether, if this general position is true, we have enough of a fact to become the basis for a valid interpretation. Tillich, as Dr. Johnson's article points out and as the present writer has heard him say, believes that the bare fact that Jesus of Nazareth historically existed is essential, but no more can be said or is necessary. But such a Christian faith would be exceedingly vulnerable to the criticism of being a fantastic illusion whose only historical fact was the statement that "Jesus of Nazareth lived." Some more facts are necessary if Christianity is going to establish itself as valid in the eyes of most people. And we have these facts.

Without repudiating what was said concerning what we do not know about the historical Jesus, the pendulum of New Testament scholarship seems to be swinging back from the extreme position. Although, unless archaeologists unearth some new and unexpected manuscripts, we can never know firsthand the details of the life of Jesus, a good deal of solid material exists which there is no reason to doubt. As Dr. Johnson's article also points out, in the New Testament there is a very real emphasis on "Jesus" as though he were a real person intimately known to some of the authors, and "unless we are to dismiss all of this as unenlightened primitive superstition . . . the conclusion is forced upon us that from its earliest beginnings the Church somehow had an unmistakable sense that in some way or other 'Jesus' plays an essential, continuing, functional part in Christian faith."[31] We know the major outlines of his adult ministry. His active ministry began with his baptism by John the Baptist. He went about as an itinerant rabbi with a remarkable teaching and preaching ability and a remarkable capacity to heal people. At first his ministry was attended by considerable success and popularity, but then the tides turned against him. After a period of withdrawal and "exile" he returned and went to Jerusalem at a Passover for a final "showdown." At Jerusalem he was betrayed by one of his own disciples and handed over to the Roman authorities on the charge of being a political revolutionist. He was put to death by crucifixion and then rose from the dead.[32]

Moreover, in spite of the above-mentioned difficulties of speaking with preciseness about the teachings of Jesus there is every reason to believe that we have the essential facts of the substance of what he taught and in many cases probably the exact words. We know that Jesus, as an itinerant rabbi, did a great deal of teaching and preaching; yet there are no real sermons recorded in the Synoptic Gospels. (The so-called Sermon on the Mount—Matt., chs. 5 to 7—is not a real sermon but a collection of sayings artificially collected by the writer. Most of the same teachings are found scattered in Luke.) What we do have are two major types of teaching: the short, pithy aphorism which frequently plays on the clever juxtaposition of words ("Judge not, that ye be not judged"), and the parable or illustration (the sower, the prodigal son, etc.). This is not surprising; this is normal expectancy. With any speaker or teacher, if we remember anything about what he said, it will be such clever aphorisms as he may have used, and his illustrations. These are precisely the types of teachings recorded in the Synoptics. We must also remember that in the time of Jesus, when few could read or write, memory was much better trained than with most of us today. Further, behind all the Gospels there are the now-lost, earlier collections of the "Sayings of Jesus," which scholars designate as Q.

A "life of Jesus" in the modern biographical sense may be "now an anachronism," but certainly we can go far farther than the minimal statement, "There was a man Jesus of Nazareth," and the information we have about him proves to be more than "unilluminating." The writer of John's Gospel declares, as has Christian faith ever since, "The Word became flesh and dwelt among us" (John 1:14). We have every reasonable reason to believe we have a good deal of factual information of the important parts of the life of the Word in that flesh (particularly in the crucial last days) and that we have the substance of what he taught. The interpretations of the Christian faith about the significance of that life rest on sufficiently factual information to make them as valid as most historical interpretations can ever be. As H. Butterfield has put it:

"Over and above all this [the facts of the historical Jesus], however, Christianity is a historical religion in a particularly technical sense that the term possesses — it presents us with religious doctrines which are at the same time historical events and historical interpretations. In particular it confronts us with questions of the incarnation, the crucifixion, and the resurrection, questions which may transcend all the apparatus of the scientific historian — as indeed many other things do — but which imply that Christianity in any of its traditional and recognizable forms has rooted its most characteristic and daring assertions in that ordinary realm of history with which the technical student is concerned." [33]

A more crucial question is: Granted that we have sufficient facts of the life of that Flesh, what right have we to believe that the Word was in it? Or, to put it another way, Why do Christians claim that the itinerant rabbi, Jesus of Nazareth, was and is the Christ? To that question we now turn.

2. Why Jesus Is the Christ

First of all in attempting to answer this question it must be admitted that in a very real sense the final answer we give rests on assumptions of faith which I have already tried to establish. In all honesty one should be fair about this. Men like Barth and Brunner are right. In the last analysis Jesus is the Christ only to faith and for faith. Without that faith Jesus is only another, perhaps remarkable, rabbi. If, however, the position taken in this book about faith and God, namely, that there is a God who created this world and all that is in it, and that he has a concern and love for men, then the *idea of a Christ* becomes a logical necessity. If there is a God who created this world and who loves and is concerned for men, and if men are inevitably caught in the dilemmas of their own finiteness and sin, then it logically follows that such a God in order to be true to his own concern would reveal his will to men in order that they might be saved from their frustrations. Since, as is clearly obvious, a man can understand nothing so well as a man who has to live the same kind of life he does, it is most logical, and normal expectancy, that God would incarnate himself in a man. Further, since it is impossible for God to take away man's freedom and still have a man, it is necessary that, on the one hand, the incarnation be sufficiently vivid to appeal and convince those who want to accept it; and, on the other hand, it must not be so overpowering as to compel acceptance. In short the logical necessity is that there be a Christ who must be decided about but who can either be accepted or rejected. It is this "logical necessity" which leads theologians like Brunner to talk about the "hidden" or "incognito" Christ. In the Synoptic Gospels, Jesus never declares himself to be the Christ (except late in his ministry and then only to his chosen few — Matt. 16: 13-20; Mark 8: 27-33; Luke 9: 18-22), yet he acts in an authoritative fashion, particularly as regards the Law which only God could alter. The idea is that if Jesus revealed his full divinity it would so overpower men that they would be compelled to accept him. This would rob them of their freedom as men. Therefore the Christ appears in Jesus "incognito."

If we grant that the Christian assumptions logically necessitate the idea of *a Christ,* there is the final question: Why do we insist that the Jewish rabbi, Jesus of Nazareth, fulfilled this requirement? Judaism, which also logically requires the idea of *a Christ,* as their prophets eventually discovered, rejects Jesus as the Christ, and, at least in orthodox Judaism, still looks for him to come. Jesus was certainly a great religious-ethical teacher but there have been other great religious-ethical teachers and practically every one of Jesus' teachings can be found given by someone else, and many of his teachings are simply paraphrases of what the rabbis were saying. He certainly lived a very noble life and died for his convictions, but happily in all ages there have been at least some men who have lived nobly and were ready to die for their convictions. These things do not make him the Christ. Why, then, do we say that Jesus was and is the Christ?

Part of the answer, as we have already indicated, is our faith, but our faith is not created out of a vacuum. There are certain facts of the " work " of Jesus which lead us with Peter to declare, " You are the Christ " (Matt. 16: 16; Mark 8: 29). I would suggest three.

A. *His Life*

As far as the records go, it is clear that *Jesus in his own life overcame the fundamental demonic contradiction in human nature and was not corrupted by his own will-to-power.* As we saw in the last chapter, all men because of the " basic givens " in human nature have an essentially selfish self-concern and will-to-power which corrupts all their idealism, and we noted how it expresses itself in various forms of resistance, even resistance to God. The remarkable, the almost uncanny thing about Jesus is that as far as the records go, he went about doing good in a purely good way without any concern for himself. Any resistance he may have felt toward God was completely overcome and he did the will of God as he saw it completely and totally. The Gospels illustrate this in many places but I would cite only two: one at the beginning and one at the end of his ministry.

The first is what is called the temptation in the wilderness. After Jesus' baptism by John the Baptist, all three Synoptics say he went off to the wilderness and was tempted by the devil. Mark merely mentions that he was " tempted by Satan " (ch. 1: 12-13), while Matthew (ch. 4: 1-11) and Luke (ch. 4: 1-12) give the details in slightly different order. For our purposes here, the order is not significant and I arbitrarily use Matthew's order. In these temptations Jesus is tempted to make bread out of stones, to throw himself down from the pinnacle of the Temple, and to worship the devil in return for world power. Each of these temptations Jesus resists, declaring in one way or another that absolute and uncompromising loyalty, obedience, and trust must be given to God alone. Why are these temptations and what is the nature of the temptations? We must remember that Jesus had just been baptized by John the Baptist and while we probably never can know all that was involved or all that it meant to Jesus it clearly constituted "a call" to serve God in more than conventional ways. He had a message to give now, but what precisely was it to be and how was he to "get it across"? The wilderness episode represents Jesus wrestling with this problem even as those of us who get a conviction wrestle with how we are to make it practical to others.

The temptations represent various ways that must have presented themselves to Jesus as methods he might use. Obviously if he had a message to give he must reach people to whom he could give it. The temptation to turn bread into stones is the temptation to solve people's physical needs first. The temptation to throw himself from the pinnacle of the Temple is the temptation to do the sensational in order to attract a crowd. The temptation to world power is the temptation to use legislation to force people to be good. When one examines these temptations critically one discovers that amazingly none of them are temptations to do evil; all of them are really temptations to do good. Sound Christian reasons can be given for any of them. In the name of Christian compassion it is important to feed people and meet their physical needs. If you have a message to give which you really believe in, it is important to get a crowd to hear it and many a church has felt justified in employing "sensational" methods such as beautiful music and elaborate pageantry. It may not be possible to legislate a person into being a Christian but most Christians in all ages have felt that the legislation of sound laws was a Christian responsibility. These are not temptations to do evil but to do good!

Why then did Jesus consider them temptations and reject them?

I think the answer is that Jesus detected in these methods two fatal flaws. One was that although they offered widely accepted methods to do good they offered them in such a way that the attention of the people would be directed to Jesus rather than to God. And, secondly, to employ them ultimately meant that Jesus was trusting in the methods and in his own ability to think them up and work them, rather than in God. In other words, he saw the basic egoistic impulse that is at the heart of all our efforts to do good and he rejected it. He was willing to trust God in a way we do not, and thus he overcame the fundamental contradiction in all human nature.

The second illustration, from the end of our Lord's life, comes from the Garden of Gethsemane episode. Again, we cannot literally recapture the precise details of that event, but it points to a momentous soul struggle—I think, the climactic decision of his earthly life. And we can recapture something of that decision. The records are clear that from every human standard of judgment the mission of Jesus had failed. Only a handful of people were loyal to him and they were confused, had only the vaguest idea what it was all about, and certainly were not anticipating his arrest. Jesus knew their pathetic state of mind and also was aware of the action of Judas. After the Last Supper, Jesus went to the Garden of Gethsemane, in a scene remarkably parallel to the temptation in the wilderness, for one last decisive struggle. Assuming, as seems justifiable, that Jesus fully understood the realities of the situation, all the arguments, both from his own natural disinclination to die and from good judgment, sound reason, and practical expediency, must have been to avoid capture and what looked like a useless death. Any reasonable person knowing the facts would have counseled him to get away, lie low until this crisis was over, go somewhere else where his message would be appreciated, at least not let himself get killed until his immediate disciples were more comprehending and better prepared and trained. The decision that Jesus faced in the Garden was whether to follow all these cogent arguments which would allow him to escape, or whether to trust God in spite of all the facts in favor of God's apparent untrustworthiness. Jesus chose to trust God in spite of both reason and personal desire. Again, he overcame the fundamental demonic contradiction in human nature and was not corrupted by his own will-to-power, will-to-pleasure, or anxiety.

We Christians have a formula for describing this attitude of our Lord in which we see him not only as a man but also as the Christ. We say, " He was tempted as we are, yet without sin." By the " yet without sin " we do not mean that Jesus never made mistakes or errors. As a man he did make mistakes and errors. At least he changed his strategy from time to time, and men do not usually change their strategy unless they think it wrong. Further, if both the story of his cleansing of the Temple (by whatever means) and the report in the Sermon on the Mount are accurate, he was inconsistent. In the Sermon on the Mount he specifically says, " Do not resist one who is evil " (Matt. 5: 39); but in the Temple he certainly did resist evil. By " yet without sin " we mean that in every place that we see Jesus he was always completely and absolutely doing the will of God as he understood it, with no thought to the consequence for himself. He *really* trusted God in a way that none of us achieve.

B. *His Death*

In his death he epitomizes the fundamentally tragic nature of all human existence.

The problem of evil and suffering is one of the most baffling problems of human existence. Volumes have been written on it and there seems to be no completely satisfactory human explanation or solution.[34] The fact of evil and suffering is an inescapable fact of existence, but the most unjust part of it is the degree to which, over and over again in history, it is the innocent that suffer unjustly for the guilty. And over all stands the inevitable end of death. No matter how good one is, or how fine and noble his intentions, when death comes that is the end. When death comes to a young person before having a chance to live we think it particularly tragic; when it comes to an older person who has had a chance to make his mark in life we have forced ourselves to be more philosophical. But that the universe should cast up any being with potentialities for hopes, dreams, and creative achievements and then snuff it out again before it can be fulfilled is fundamentally unjust. There is some truth in that cynic of the Old Testament, Ecclesiastes: "Again I saw that under the sun the race is not to the swift, nor the battle to the strong, nor bread to the wise, nor riches to the intelligent, nor favor to the men of skill; but time and chance happen to them all. . . . Like fish which are taken in an evil net, and like birds which are caught in a snare, so the sons of men are snared at an evil time, when it suddenly falls upon them. . . . For the fate of the sons of men and the fate of beasts is the same; as one dies, so dies the other. . . . All go to one place; all are from the dust, and all turn to dust again." (Eccl. 9: 11-12; 3: 19-20.) This is the kind of world we live in, and to pretend that it is otherwise is both stupid and superficial.

In the light of these facts of human existence let us now consider the life of Jesus. For the moment, if we set aside any claims of divinity and consider him simply as a human being, Jesus was a good man. Some would say the best who ever lived. If that is too extravagant, he certainly belongs in that little select company of the world's finest people. At a minimal estimate he was a *really* good man. As a good man, if there is any real justice in this world, Jesus ought to have lived to a ripe old age and died in bed with his friends about him. In fact, if he were really good and if life were just, he ought not to have died at all, for the extinction of goodness is a loss to all life and therefore unjust. (Therefore Christians claim that although Jesus died he was raised from the dead—but see more below.) But Jesus not only died early as a relatively young man, he also died a very cruel and the most degradingly criminal death that the Roman Empire could devise. Thus we have the picture of the really good man and the innocent man being unjustly put to death by the combined forces of evil. And if any further evidence of the tragic injustice of life is needed, it is significant that some of those "forces of evil" that killed Jesus were sincere men who honestly thought they were doing the right thing.

Jesus, in his life and death, symbolizes, epitomizes, and illumines the tragic and unjust nature of human life. And apparently Jesus thought it was unjust too. At least according to Mark and Matthew in his last agony on the cross he cried, "My God, my God, why hast thou forsaken me?" (Mark 15:34; Matt. 27:46). Mr. H. G. Wells once wrote that these words "echo down the ages, a perpetual riddle to the faithful,"[35] but then Mr. Wells was not very profound in his understanding of Christianity. In some ways this agonized cry of despair from the cross is the greatest thing our Lord ever said. For in this cry Jesus not only reveals the tragic nature of life — all men at one time or another cry this cry in their own words — he reveals that he too enters into the depths of human despair and doubt. It is here more than anywhere else that he touches us and actually gets involved in the kind of life we men and women have to live. But it is more than a revelation of what life is like — it is a revelation that God himself, through Jesus who is the Christ, enters into and shares the depths of human despair. There is no unjust tragedy which can befall a person in which that person cannot discover that Jesus Christ was there before him and is there with him. The importance of this cannot be overestimated. (It is significant that in some of their forms the early Christian heresies of Docetism and Gnosticism claimed that the divine Christ left the human Jesus before the crucifixion. Christian orthodoxy rightly condemned this as heresy, for it robs Christianity of one of its most essential points. Modern "gnostics" who also deny the divinity of Christ do not realize what they are saying about God and the problems of evil.) Life as we have to live it is rough, tough, and frequently unjust. In the end all of us have to go "through the valley of the shadow of death" (Ps. 23:4). It makes all the difference in the world for us whether or not the God who created the universe enters into and shares this tragic life and death with us. Christianity says he does and that in Jesus we see a revelation of what the ultimate nature of life is like, including not only the tragedy, but God's voluntary sharing it.

C. *His Resurrection*

In his resurrection Jesus is the historical guarantee of the ultimate victory of God (and man when he is with God) over all the powers of evil in human existence.

If it is possible to say there is one aspect of the Christian faith that is more important than any other, then the resurrection is it. Without the resurrection there would have been no Christianity. As any careful reading of the New Testament will indicate, the Graeco-Roman world was not converted to Christianity on the basis of the ethical teachings of Jesus, nor on the nobility of his life or death; it was converted on the message: "This Jesus, delivered up according to the definite plan and foreknowledge of God, you crucified and killed by the hands of lawless men. But God raised him up" (Acts 2:23-24). Paul, in his famous fifteenth chapter of First Corinthians, makes the position even more emphatic: "If Christ has not been raised, then our preaching is in vain and your faith is in vain. . . . If Christ has not been raised, your faith is futile and you are still in your sins. . . . If in this life we who are in Christ have only hope [but not the fact], we are of all men most to be pitied." (Vs. 14, 17, 19.) This is strong language — but not too strong! It is in the resurrection of Jesus, more than any one place, that Christianity and its faith that Jesus is the Christ stands or falls.

The resurrection, then, is the *sine qua non* of Christian faith; but it is the resurrection which causes the greatest difficulty for modern people. Admittedly the resurrection of Jesus Christ defies all the known scientific laws of life and nature. Many people quite honestly do not see how it could happen and therefore they reject it as a fantasy or hallucination of the early Christians which can no longer be accepted at its face value. If some of these people remain "Christians" for other reasons, they try to side-step the question of the resurrection, or interpret it as some "ongoing spirit of good will." But the resurrection, if reduced to an "ongoing spirit of good will," has had the heart and real meaning taken out of it. In view of these difficulties what genuine evidence is there for the fact of the resurrection?

As was noted at the beginning of this chapter, when we are dealing with historical facts of nearly two thousand years ago we are limited to the reports of the people who observed the events and these reports are unquestionably colored both by the experience of the reporters and by our own prejudices in accepting or rejecting them. In a strictly scientific sense there is no incontrovertible proof that Jesus rose from the dead. There is no way *to prove* that the various resurrection stories reported in the Gospels are not inventions. We know these stories were written a generation or more after the event. In view of the New Testament writers' penchant for parable and symbol and their obvious purpose to win converts, each of the resurrection stories is suspect in its literal aspects. The only resurrection story that appears in all the Gospels is the story of the empty tomb, which does not prove that Jesus rose from the dead. It only proves, if it proves anything, that the tomb was empty. Jesus' disciples might have stolen his body as is hinted in Matt. 27: 62-64, and this story has the earmarks of having been "written back," that is, having been written to explain an objection that arose after the event reported.

There is no absolute proof in the modern scientific sense of that term that Jesus either did or did not rise from the dead. In the last analysis belief in the resurrection does rest on faith, but again it is not "blind faith in a vacuum." There is a good deal of solid evidence which makes that faith reasonable — as reasonable as our belief that any other event took place in the ancient world. Let us consider this evidence.

First of all, a theoretic point that is not inconsequential. If there is a God in anything like the Christian sense which we have maintained, that is, a God who created this universe and all that is in it, including man, then the matter of raising a man from the dead ought to be a relatively simple thing for such a God. I sometimes meet people who say they can believe in God but not in the resurrection. This seems to me getting the cart before the horse. Actually, it seems to me, that belief in God is much more difficult, but once belief in a God who is God is accepted, belief in the resurrection rather naturally follows. Further, if the whole general position maintained in the preceding chapters of this book is true, namely, that not only is there a God but that he has created man whom he loves, yet these men are doomed to death, then it logically follows that it is normal expectancy that God would provide some means for solving the problem of death. This is especially true of Jesus. The speech attributed to Peter in Acts, ch. 2, draws an absolutely logical conclusion, " But God raised him up, having loosed the pangs of death, because it was not possible for him to be held by it " (v. 24); for if God is really God, it is impossible that the really good can be permanently destroyed. As Harry Emerson Fosdick has pointed out,[36] the Christian belief in the resurrection is not an isolated belief, it is part of a whole family of beliefs all of which are bound together. When seen in this context it becomes justifiable to say that if God did not raise Jesus from the dead, he ought to have in order to be consistent with his other revelations.

To turn from the theoretical to the historical: we have seen that all the resurrection stories in the Gospels are, at best, second- or third-hand accounts and each is somewhat suspect. There is, however, in the New Testament some solid firsthand evidence and that is in Paul's first letter to the Corinthians. No reputable scholar denies that this is a genuine letter of Paul and that we are confronted with firsthand testimony. Paul writes:

> " For I delivered to you as of first importance what I also received, that Christ died for our sins in accordance with the scriptures, that he was buried, that he was raised on the third day in accordance with the scriptures, and that he appeared to Cephas [Peter], then to the twelve. Then he appeared to more than five hundred brethren at one time, most of whom are still alive, though some have fallen asleep. Then he appeared to James, then to all the apostles. Last of all, as to one ultimately born, he appeared also to me." (I Cor. 15: 3-8.)

Paul here is listing actual people whom he knows personally who have had experiences of the risen Christ. In this statement he is simply corroborating the testimony of all of the New Testament. It does not matter which book you read; every one of them in one way or another points to the utterly amazing, world-shaking event that God raised Jesus from the dead. This is true not only of the speeches in Acts, the Pauline letters, and of the non-Pauline letters, it is equally true of the Gospels. Some moderns, anxious to preserve the life and teachings of Jesus and escape the resurrection, have turned to the Gospels as authoritative but, oddly, only up to the crucifixion. The resurrection stories are considered unimportant. This is a gross distortion of the intent of the Gospel writers. Every one of their accounts of the life of Jesus leads up to the resurrection as the climax which validates all that has gone before.[37] When we put all this evidence together, both the direct and the indirect testimony, the total effect is to make the New Testament testimony to the historical validity of the resurrection convincing to anyone, unless he deliberately chooses to reject it for other reasons.

Granting then that the historical fact of the resurrection is as safely established as the facts about almost any man in ancient history, what was the nature of the resurrection? This is an important question because many people who would like to believe in the resurrection cannot accept it in a literal physical sense. The New Testament does not require that we believe in the physical resurrection in the normal meaning of the word "physical."

The place where the New Testament has the fullest discussion of the nature of the resurrection is in I Cor., ch. 15, especially vs. 36-58. Here Paul speaks about the resurrection of the body in an extended argument, but he makes clear, even in the English translation, that the resurrected body is completely different from what we normally mean by a physical flesh-and-blood body. "So it is with the resurrection of the dead. What is sown is perishable, what is raised is imperishable. It is sown in dishonor, it is raised in glory. . . . It is sown a physical body, it is raised a spiritual body. . . . I tell you this, brethren: flesh and blood cannot inherit the kingdom of God." (Vs. 42-44, 50.) [38] The position taken here is in line with the rest of the New Testament. If we examine carefully the firsthand testimony given above where Paul lists the people he knows personally as having witnessed the resurrection, he concludes, "Last of all, as to one untimely born, he appeared also to me" (v. 8). The clear implication is that Paul thinks of his experience of the resurrection as of the same nature as all the others.

The key, then, to understanding the nature of the resurrection is in Paul's experience on the road to Damascus and this is reported four times in the New Testament, three times in The Acts and once more briefly in Galatians. The Galatian account is the only firsthand account and it gives none of the details, although as we shall see in a moment, there is one significant verse. The Acts, including the speeches put in the mouths of various people, was written by Luke, so even the three accounts in The Acts where Paul is speaking of his resurrection experience are really secondhand. However, we must remember that Luke was Paul's traveling companion. He must have known Paul intimately and heard Paul tell his story many times. Consequently Luke's stories in The Acts must be accurate in substance if not in exact wording. When we examine these stories we find that, except for slightly different wording and differences as to how much Paul's companions were aware of what happened, all are similar. Their slight differences give an added note of authenticity. In these stories it is quite clear that Paul alone had an experience of the risen Christ. His traveling companions knew that something had happened to Paul; it is suggested that they knew something had happened around them, but they did not share his experience. In other words, Paul's experience was *essentially subjective*. His own brief account in Galatians further substantiates the subjective nature of his experience: "But when he who had set me apart . . . was pleased to reveal his Son *in* me" (ch. 1:15-16).[39] It is quite likely that Paul in II Cor. 4:6 is actually describing the nature of that experience: "For it is the God who said, 'Let light shine out of darkness,' who has shone in our hearts to give the light of the knowledge of the glory of God in the face of Christ."

Thus, whether we examine either Paul's discussion of the nature of the resurrection or the reports of his own experience of the resurrected Christ, we find that in neither case does it presuppose a physical body as an objective physical entity—one, say, that could be photographed if anyone had been there with a camera. Rather, all the evidence points to the fact that it was a private, subjective experience. Since, as we have seen, Paul explicitly equates his experience with those of the others and since there is absolutely no evidence that he was ever challenged on this crucial point, it seems logical to conclude that all the resurrection experiences were subjective (although some of them were doubtless group experiences). This does *not* mean that they were any less real or genuine. One of the places where the acids of modernity have been most corrosive is in the insistence that all true knowledge must be objective and that subjective knowledge or experience is fantasy. Actually the only experience that is a real experience for the individual is one which he appropriates and feels in himself, that is, subjectively. As Kierkegaard once observed, "One does not become a hero or a lover objectively."[40] The fact that the resurrection experiences recorded in the New Testament were subjective means that they were the only real, historical, and valid experiences there could be and still be genuine experiences.

One last point in connection with these stories needs to be considered. The individual resurrection stories as they appear in the Gospels are portrayed in vivid detail, and the resurrected Christ is portrayed as fulfilling many of the characteristics of a normal physical person. He walks, talks, eats, and, in the story of doubting Thomas orders Thomas to feel his wounds (John 20:26-29). Only in the story of Mary Magdalene mistaking Jesus for the gardener (John 20:11-18) is there a suggestion that Jesus is a "ghostly figure" ("Jesus said to her, 'Do not hold me, for I have not yet ascended to the Father'"—v. 17). How are we to explain this vivid physical detail? As is pointed out in the chapter on the Bible, the Biblical writers were not slaves of literalism. They were imaginative storytellers who knew, as any good storyteller does, that the point of a story is more important than the details. With a clear conscience they were quite ready to embroider, or even invent, if that would make the point more vivid and compelling. The Gospel writers, indeed all of the early Christians, had had an overwhelming experience of the risen Christ. It was the most real fact of their lives and it had completely changed their lives. In their knowledge that God had raised Christ from the dead they had received a whole new world-changing understanding of human life and destiny which gave them an undreamed-of joy and confidence. They wanted others to understand this too. Consequently they told these stories of this experience in the most vivid and concrete fashion they could in order to make others believe what they knew to be the truth.

Thus, on the basis of the New Testament evidence the resurrection of Jesus from the dead was not a resurrection of a physical body in the usual meaning of that term, but it was a genuine resurrection which happened in history and was witnessed by a number of people whose testimony there is no good reason to doubt. And it is this fact of the resurrection more than any other one thing which convinces us Christians that Jesus of Nazareth was in some unique way the incarnation of God, God's revealer in a way no other man has been — in a word, that he was the Christ, the bringer of new hope and new life to mankind.

CHAPTER

VI

The Significance of Jesus Who Is the Christ

1. The Resurrection — Personal

If the fact and the nature of the resurrection have been established, then the most important question is, What is its meaning and its significance, especially for the ordinary living of ordinary people?

Obviously the most common understanding of the meaning of the resurrection is the assurance of eternal life, more especially, personal survival after death. However, the Christian understanding of the meaning of eternal life which is guaranteed in the resurrection is far more inclusive than just our personal survival, although that of course is included of necessity. We shall discuss this in a moment, but first there are some other matters to clear up.

In discussing the matter of life after death the most popular term today is "immortality," or "immortality of the soul." Since it is the common terminology I suppose it cannot be abandoned, but strictly speaking, the Bible does not speak of "immortality of the soul"; rather, it speaks of "resurrection of the dead." The idea of "immortality" is essentially a Greek rather than a Biblical idea, and it is derived from a combination of Greek speculative thinking (philosophy) and of human arrogance. The Greeks claimed that there was that in man which was divine and eternal and it was too good to be destroyed; consequently this divine part of man, usually called the soul, was immortal and continued on beyond death.[41] This conception is very flattering to men's egos and most people want to believe it. Except for the relatively few suicides who find life so intolerable that they think anything would be preferable, all people want to live. All of us for whom life is good at all want to continue to live and fear our complete extinction. Those who say they do not are either kidding themselves or they have, perhaps unconsciously, stoically disciplined themselves to accept the inevitable. The idea of immortality gives people what they want to believe and flatters their egos at the same time. But there is no proof of immortality, as Socrates, whose argument for it has never been beaten, readily admitted.

The Biblical conception of death and resurrection is more realistic and profound. It does not pretend that we can comfort ourselves by easy arguments of ongoing goodness. As Paul Tillich writes: "Do not deceive yourself about the seriousness of death — not death in general, not somebody else's death, but your own death — by nice arguments for immortality of the soul. The Christian message is more realistic than those arguments."[42] Biblical Christianity faces without evasion the fact that death is real and that when we are dead we are really dead. It is significant that both the Gospels and the Creeds insist that Jesus not only was crucified, but also that he died *and he was buried*. Because of our fear of death and our desire for immortality we have avoided facing the full implications of this realism. But Karl Barth pregnantly recalls us to the facts:

"Death really means the *end*. . . . To be born and grow up, to ripen and grow old is to go toward the moment at which for each of us it will be the end, definitely the end. . . . Someday we shall be buried. Someday a company of men will process out to a church yard and lower a coffin and everyone will go home; but one will never come back, and that will be me. . . . Perhaps a memory will remain, so long as there are men who like to remember me. But someday they too will die and this memory too will pass away. There is no great name in human history which will not someday or other have become a forgotten name. That is the meaning of being "buried," . . . that in the grave [man] drops into forgottenness."[43]

Strictly speaking then, Biblical Christianity does not speak about the "immortality of the soul"; it speaks of death, which is then followed by resurrection. Actually none of us knows what happens on the other side of death. We are all confounded by the question asked of Job, "Have the gates of death been revealed to you, or have you seen the gates of deep darkness?" (Job 38:17), and we must answer with Job, "I have uttered what I did not understand, things too wonderful for me, which I did not know" (Job 42:3). Any statement about after death is only provisional, tentative, and symbolic. In a personal letter to the author, Dr. Paul Tillich writes:

"Do not take *any* symbol of 'eternal life' literally. They are all highly symbolic. I would even deny the continuity of existence after death *as an event in time and space,* because eternity is the transcending of time and space (although as their creative ground not as their complete negation). . . . If one uses symbolic statements about man's eternal destiny, the *central* symbol is 'eternal life.' Secondary symbols are: Immortality (victory over death); Resurrection of the body (eternal meaning of the individuality expressed in the body, but in no way a continuation of *this* body or the appearance of another body in terms of *spatial* existence); Reincarnation (pointing to the imperfect state at the moment of death); mystical Union (pointing to the return into the Creative Ground). Each word is equally adequate and inadequate: it is symbolic and pointing, *not* descriptive. The heaven is not a place, and the 'body of the resurrection' is not subject to the categories of space. Otherwise we confuse pictorial imaginations (medieval paintings) with ontological thought. Only one point I want to stress: The continuation of 'ghostly souls,' if taken literally, is not less superstitious than the rising of dead bodies." (Italics Dr. Tillich's.)

The only place where I would disagree with this statement is in claiming that "eternal life" is "the central symbol." We know nothing of what goes on beyond the grave, except that we know that God raised Jesus Christ from the dead. Beyond that fact everything we say including affirming "eternal life" is at best human speculation and at worst wish thinking. We can only really affirm "eternal life" because of what God has revealed in

Jesus Christ. Therefore the " central symbol " is " death and resurrection," and because God raised our Lord Jesus Christ from the dead we know that a " life " beyond this is a reality. This then is one significance of the resurrection which is not inconsiderable; for an individual's own life is tremendously important to him, and to snuff it out arbitrarily with no hope of fulfillment is patently unjust.

2. The Resurrection and the Problem of Evil

But the significance of the resurrection is far greater than just the guarantee of the individual's personal survival, although that of necessity is included. After all, I may personally want to survive, but to insist that I ought to survive, or that I must survive, has in it an unjustifiable element of personal arrogance and egotism. Actually, my survival or resurrection is only important because it is part of a much larger question: the solution of the problem of evil and suffering.

Another significance of the resurrection is that it offers the only solution to the problem of evil that there is. As we have noted above, the problem of evil and suffering is the most baffling problem there is — at least for anyone who attempts to make any sense out of life. Yet, for some strange reason, most of us refuse to face the enormity of suffering until we ourselves are actually caught by it. The simple fact is that the amount of unjust suffering and evil there is in the world — and always has been — is simply incalculably appalling. It is so appalling that many, many people do not see how there can be a good God who permits such evil.

One of the oldest and most revered explanations is that God, wanting man to be really a man with character, gave man freedom of choice. From some points of view a lot can be said for this explanation. Certainly if there is any one thing that makes man a man and not just an automaton it is his capacity to make free choices (at least free within limits as noted above). And character is a meaningless term unless man deliberately chooses the good when he could have chosen the evil. But this line of argument, namely, that God permits evil in order that men may choose the good and develop character, while it has some validity, is not completely satisfactory. In fact there are some glaring weaknesses in it. In the first place, although it is true that some temptations to do evil, when resisted, do produce character, it is also true, as every social worker knows, that for some people the temptations and evil are so great that they destroy character rather than build it. In the second place, this argument presupposes that all the evil and suffering in the world is the result of bad human choices. A tremendous amount of human suffering is unquestionably the result of "man's inhumanity to man," but by no means all of it. Much of it is the result of natural causes for which no person can be held morally responsible—such things as disease, floods, famines, accidents, etc. To say that all these natural evils are necessary to produce character is superficial. That a hundred thousand people should die in a famine or an earthquake in order to produce a handful of noble characters who arise above their adversity is an unjust and immoral price to pay. In the third place, nobody asked to be born! None of us were asked first if we wanted to enter this life of human finiteness with its terrific burdens of responsibilities and decisions. None of us volunteered to be tested in this crucible. The choice was not ours; it was forced upon us and the conditions that we have to accept include our own inadequacy to do the job perfectly. In this sense the responsibility for our lives and for our right decisions is not completely ours and there is some justice in the bitter lines:

> "O Thou, who Man of baser Earth didst make,
> And e'en with Paradise devise the Snake:
> For all the Sin wherewith the Face of Man
> Is blackened—Man's forgiveness give—and take!" [44]

For all these reasons the answer that God created evil simply to test men's characters and help them grow is less than satisfactory; and when one compares the amount of suffering there always has been in the world, and which still exists, with the results, all but the most superficial must declare that the price is not worth it. If that is the best God can do, he must be nearer a fiend than the God revealed in our Lord Jesus Christ.

There is no completely satisfactory answer to the question why there is evil. We can explain why there are some particular evils and perhaps whole classes of them, but not the basic question of why a good God should create a world with so much evil and suffering as ours obviously has. One of the most popular attempts to answer this problem is to claim that God is only a finite and limited God—he is good but not powerful enough. He too has to struggle with evil or with some force or stuff which makes for evil. In the noblest exponents of this position man is called on to co-operate and help God in the struggle. Such a position has many attractive features, particularly from the human point of view, for it gives man a very heroic and semidivine role; but from a Christian point of view it is untenable. The position presupposes a force or power of evil which is independent of God, and in that case God is not really God and the creator of the universe. Further, if there is an independent power of evil which God did not create and with which he must contend, there is always the possibility that he may fail (with or without human help), in which case he is something far short of the Biblical concept of God who quite definitely is Lord of Creation and "whose purposes falter not, neither are stayed." Consequently, whatever the philosopher may do, the Christian cannot accept the thesis of a limited and finite God as an explanation of the fact of evil.

Whatever the solution to the question of evil, the Christian must find it within the context of Isa. 45:7: "I form the light, and create darkness; I make peace, and create evil; I am Jehovah, that doeth all these things" (ARV). See also Amos 3:6, which maintains the "Godship" (if I may coin a word) of God. Such a position places a heavier burden on us Christians, but it may lead to a more profound understanding.

For the moment, let us leave off trying to explain "the why" of evil. It is an interesting academic point and makes for fascinating argument, but the simple fact remains that whatever explanation we may arrive at, or none at all, evil does exist. Evil and suffering are facts of our lives which none of us escapes. There are those, notably the Christian Scientists, who claim that evil does not exist and it is simply an illusion of our minds and bad thinking. I am willing to admit that philosophically everything we know or experience can be reduced to an illusion of the mind, but as a friend of mine once put it, "If I cross the street and get hit by a truck, it may all be an illusion but as far as I am concerned it is a devastating illusion!" Speaking practically, evil is a fact of life and the real problem is not so much explaining the why as it is learning how to live with it, cope with it, and triumph over it.

It is at this point that the Christian doctrines of the incarnation, crucifixion, and resurrection, which are inseparably bound together, become relevant to the practical problem of living. They offer the only adequate solution to the problem of evil that there is.

Jesus, as we have seen, was the really good man who was unjustly and cruelly put to criminal death. Perhaps in spite of, perhaps because of, the traditional church celebrations at Good Friday and Easter, it is awfully hard for us to recapture the genuine tragedy, agony, and despair of his crucifixion. Crucifixion was a slow, tortuous death, and even if Jesus lasted only three hours, it was a terrible three hours. But Jesus' agony and despair must have been far greater than just the physical pain, great as that must have been. Jesus had confidently preached that "the kingdom of God is at hand," and not only had the Kingdom not come, but also his friends had deserted him and his plans and hopes seemed utterly wrecked. His faith must have seemed a horrible illusion. On top of all this disillusionment was the weight of exhaustion and sheer physical pain. And Jesus cried out (what many scholars believe is the only authentic one of the traditional "Seven Last Words"), "My God, my God, why hast thou forsaken me?" (Matt. 27:46; Mark 15:34). In other words, in his extremity Jesus touched the rock-bottom depth of hopeless despair, and even doubted the goodness of God. Beyond this, it is impossible to go. And Christianity placards this hopeless despair of its Lord for all to see! It does so for two very significant reasons. One is that because of the incarnation (as we shall see in a moment) Christianity faces life realistically. It attempts neither to deny, minimize, nor evade the full weight of the reality of evil. It states unequivocally: Yes! Life can be so unjust, so bad, so defeating that even from our Lord there was forced the cry, "My God, my God, why hast thou forsaken me?" No other philosophy faces the problem of evil more honestly; no other religion has dared to portray its lord in the same realistic colors. The second reason is implicit in the resurrection. Because of the resurrection, and only because of the resurrection, the Christian knows that evil (the crucifixion), even when it seems completely defeating, even when it forces temporarily a doubt about God, is not the final word. The final word and the final triumph is in the resurrection, which overcame the evil of the cross. And since the resurrection is something no man can do, it is the ultimate revelation of God and of both his power and purpose to overcome evil.

3. The Incarnation

All this offers a twofold solution to the problem of evil. The first involves the incarnation. For reasons we have already considered, Christianity insists that God was really in Jesus of Nazareth so that he was Christ incarnate. The incarnation, at least in the New Testament sense, has been a difficulty for many moderns. The Christian claim that Jesus of Nazareth was both fully God and fully man seems impossible to logical rational thought. Admittedly there is a mystery here that goes beyond logical thought and the Church has never pretended it was otherwise; but the Church has not insisted on the two natures of Christ and labeled all attempts to change or modify its insistence as heresies, merely to be difficult. If God was not in Christ, one of the important "handles" for dealing with the problem of evil is destroyed. Because of the incarnation, Christianity insists that, whatever the cause or reason for evil and suffering may be, God himself does not leave man to struggle and bear his suffering alone; God enters into the depths of it and shares it, paradoxically and mysteriously even to the point of sharing human doubt about God. No human being can enter a situation of despair, doubt, or suffering which God in Christ has not already entered! Such knowledge, while it neither explains nor reduces evil, does give us a confidence and power in dealing with evil which we otherwise would not have. This is why the incarnation is so important. If I may paraphrase Paul's great statement in Phil. 2:8: "And having become just like any other human being, he obediently humbled himself to the tragedy of the human situation even to a death like that of a Gestapo torture chamber." People who attempt to minimize or bypass the incarnation have never seriously faced the problem of evil.

The second solution to the problem of evil involves the resurrection, which is one of the reasons, perhaps the main reason, for believing in the incarnation. (Ordinary human beings do not raise themselves from the dead.) This needs less elaboration, for it has already been suggested. According to the Christian faith the ultimate revelation of God is in the resurrection. The resurrection is the victory over death, and "the last enemy to be destroyed is death" (I Cor. 15:26). Paul states it this way because he understands that death, which is the complete and total frustration of all human hopes, desires, and ambitions, symbolizes and epitomizes all the frustrations of life — thus it symbolizes the ultimate expression of evil. In other words, we know that because of the resurrection evil does not triumph in the long run. In this world and in our lives it does triumph (that is what the realism of the crucifixion admits), but we are citizens of two worlds, of which this world, although more real to us now, is ultimately the less important. From the eternal perspective which understands man's total situation and destiny, God has revealed in the resurrection of Jesus Christ that evil is doomed and good will triumph. "For I am sure that neither death, nor life, nor angels, nor principalities, nor things present, nor things to come, nor height, nor depth, *nor anything else in all creation,* will be able to separate us from the love of God in Christ Jesus our Lord." (Rom. 8:38-39.)

4. The Basis of Ethics

Many moderns (and indeed many of the ancients too) criticize this Christian supranaturalism and "otherworldliness" on the ground that as far as trying to improve this world is concerned, it is defeating and that it cuts the nerve of social action. In all honesty it must be sadly admitted that some Christians by their attitudes and actions—or lack of action—have given solid ground for this accusation. At this point we Christians must simply confess our sins. It is always easier to profess rightly than it is to act courageously, particularly when it involves risks, and although Christians are not alone in failing in this regard we are tarred with that brush.

All too often Christians have used our "otherworldly" hope as an escape device from honestly facing and doing something about the injustices of this world. But such an interpretation of the Christian position does not necessarily follow and it actually is a distortion of the meaning and implication of our faith. Properly understood, Christian supranaturalism and "otherworldliness," particularly as revealed in the resurrection, gives the strongest foundation for ethical action that there is.

"So faith, hope, love abide," wrote Paul, "these three; but the greatest of these is love." (I Cor. 13:13.) Love may be the greatest, because faith and hope can be expressed only in love, but, and this is often forgotten, there cannot be any abiding love where there is not faith and hope. In this context we are thinking of love primarily in its social and ethical implications, namely, the motive to try to battle evil, work for justice, and make our world a better, happier place to live for all people. The simple fact is that people will not work at any cause for any length of time unless they believe either that the cause will ultimately succeed, or that in working for it they are identifying themselves with that which will ultimately succeed even though the particular cause fails. Some people say they try to do "the right" simply because it is right and that is the only justification they need. Such people have not analyzed the situation with sufficient penetration. On further analysis such people try to do the right because they believe there is a Something—perhaps a "structure of the universe" (it is usually unthought-out and many of these people would object to the word "God")—but anyway, "a Something" in the world, which means that to do the right is to be on "the better" and ultimately winning side. If they did not believe this, they would not act as they do. Any person who has completely lost faith and hope has also lost the capacity to love, and he is in complete despair.

Now this blind faith in an indefinite "Something" that supports the good has its noble aspects, and it may be part of the general grace of God given even to those who deny him. But actually there is nothing in the world that justifies such a faith unless one first posits a God either who is "the Something" or else who stands back of it and guarantees it. And certainly, *except for the resurrection, nothing in history justifies such a faith.* History reveals an endless struggle going on between good and evil. From a particular perspective sometimes one seems to gain the upper hand temporarily and sometimes the other, but it is all very mixed up. From our point of view, we who believe in freedom and democracy are "good," and those periods of history which approximated these goals are "good periods"; but from the communist or fascist point of view, what we consider good is the source of all evil. If in every age there are saints, so also in every age "the wicked prosper," and more frequently than not the saints come to a "bad end" and the wicked go on prospering. Nowhere do we see in human experience a clean-cut absolute victory of good over evil—a sufficiently absolute one to justify the faith that there is an undefeatable Something in the structure of the universe which makes for righteousness—except in the resurrection of our Lord Jesus Christ.

It is in the historical fact of the resurrection that we have revealed to us the ultimate nature of human destiny—*that the end is in the hands of God and therefore that the end is good.* The whole crucifixion-resurrection story is particularly instructive at this point, for it reveals the ambiguity of all human efforts to achieve the good. We must remember that the men who delivered Jesus to Pilate and clamored for his death were not evil men, but good men for the most part, sincerely trying to do what they believed was good for themselves, their nation, and their religion. While all men's motives are mixed, most of the Jewish leaders sincerely believed Jesus was a blasphemer who was breaking their sacred and God-given law (as indeed he was), and that if he was allowed to go on, not only might he destroy all they believed was good, but also, if he got a real following, as seemed likely, he would force the Roman Government to act drastically (John 11:47-48). As has happened so many, many times both before and since, at the crucifixion evil was done by good men trying to do what they thought was right. The crucifixion stands for the fact of human experience that the good is so often destroyed by the combined forces of evil, paradoxically and tragically some of them intending to do the good. If this is a true picture of life, and I think any unflinching appraisal must admit it is, there is no basis for any ethics of any sort, Christian or otherwise, except expediency and adjusting to shifting relative conventions of the moment.

It is a very significant fact that in the twentieth century when there is widespread doubt about the truth of the Christian faith there are at the same time two major ethical developments. One is the amazing increase in philosophies of ethical relativity, and the other is the amazing acceptance of the absoluteness of the state to establish ethical norms. These developments are not accidental. The twentieth century has shattered the Enlightenment faith in the goodness of man and has largely lost the Christian faith in the goodness of a God who overcame the crucifixion. With these gone, what else is there for man to cling to? Man cannot live, much less love, without faith and hope in something. The less intellectual turn to nationalism and the authority of the state; the intellectuals develop very rational philosophies of relative ethics, for the intellectuals are smart enough to see that in history there is no permanent victory of the good and that what is called good in one society is called evil in another. But neither suffices. As we have only too tragically seen in our time, the more absolute the state becomes the more it destroys men, even the men who helped create it. And the philosophy of relativity is really the destroyer of ethics, for why stand for anything in particular at the cost of some self-sacrifice when it is all going to change in a little while anyway?

If the command of ethics is to love — to fight for what is right, to try to transform injustice, and to bring decency and true humanness where there is indecency, particularly at some, perhaps great, personal cost and self-sacrifice — a man has to believe that this action is commanded and guaranteed by something that is really permanent in the universe — by a God who is good and who can overcome evil. Nowhere in history do we see this actually demonstrated outside of the resurrection. If the resurrection did not take place, Paul is right, "our preaching is in vain and your faith is in vain" and "we are of all men most to be pitied" (I Cor. 15:14, 19). But God raised Jesus Christ from the dead after the forces of evil had done their utmost. In that demonstration we have a solid basis for faith and hope in the ultimate victory of the good — and so we can love even if it means our defeat in this world.

The Christian doctrine of the resurrection admittedly involves the supranatural and the otherworldly, indeed it is impossible to explain without them, but it does not necessarily nor properly lead to the kind of otherworldliness that cuts the nerve of ethical action. Properly understood the resurrection is the *sine qua non* and the only solid basis there is for ethical action.

5. The Atonement

One last, and perhaps the most significant, aspect of the work of our Lord needs to be considered, and that is *the atonement*. Of all the major Christian doctrines, in twentieth-century America at least, the doctrine of the atonement has gone into the greatest eclipse. Happily there is some evidence of a renewed interest in this great indispensable Christian doctrine, but among the rank and file of the laity and of many of the clergy, its significance is not understood.

The cause for the eclipse of the atonement in Christian thought and preaching is not hard to find. The religious thinking of the first part of the twentieth century was largely informed by nineteenth-century optimism about the nature of man. When man is thought of as essentially good and it is believed that his major problem is ignorance (rather than sin) which can be overcome by "right education," the doctrine of the atonement inevitably seems superfluous. In fact, it is more than superfluous, it is insulting to human dignity, for the doctrine of the atonement only makes sense on the assumption that man is a sinner incapable of saving himself, and that in order "to be saved" something drastic and beyond human ingenuity has to be done. This is what, at least until relatively recently, we have not wanted to believe about ourselves. If, however, what has been said in Chapter IV about man is true, then a doctrine of atonement becomes an absolute necessity.

The doctrine of the atonement arises through logical necessity out of three other basic assumptions of the Christian faith: the goodness of God, the sinfulness of man, and the faith that God, as man's creator, loves and wants to reconcile man to himself. In order that there can be a genuine reconciliation between a perfect God and a sinful man who is incapable of overcoming his sin by himself, something drastic — something "beyond man" — has to happen. It is the Christian faith that this "something drastic" happened in the crucifixion of Jesus, who is Christ.

Perhaps the most dramatic place where this event is described in the Gospels is in Matthew, where, after describing the death of Jesus, it says, "And behold, the curtain of the temple was torn in two, from top to bottom" (Ch. 27:51). The innermost sanctuary of the Temple at Jerusalem was a small, isolated building in the Inner Court. It was known as the Holy of Holies, and although the Hebrews believed God could and did operate anywhere, the Holy of Holies in some special way was his unique dwelling place. So sacred was this place that no one could ever enter it except the high priest once a year (and then only after special purification on the Day of Atonement). Across the door of the Holy of Holies was a curtain — it is called " veil " in the older translations. This curtain was a kind of " spiritual iron curtain " which perpetually separated a Holy and Perfect God from the eyes and contamination of sinful men. When Matthew says that at Jesus' death " the curtain of the temple was torn in two " he does not mean as we noted in Chapter II that if anyone had had a modern camera and had taken a photograph of the curtain that afternoon he would have found the curtain torn in the picture. Rather, he means, and Christian faith has always understood, that somehow by his death on the cross our Lord destroyed " the curtain " that separated sinful man from his Holy God. Christ by his death did the " drastic something " that man could not do himself and made possible the reconciliation and " at-one-ment " of God and man. " But now in Christ Jesus you who once were far off have been brought near in the blood [crucifixion] of Christ. For he is our peace, who has made us both one, and has broken down the dividing wall of hostility." (Eph. 2:13, 14.)

The doctrine of the atonement tries to express a fact of Christian faith and experience, namely, that in spite of the sinfulness and unworthiness of man, man can be reconciled to God because of God's concern and action. But when it comes to explaining in a neat formula just exactly what happened in the atonement the Church has always been baffled. There is a mystery here that defies neat human formulation, and at one time or another there have been various theories of the atonement. None of them have been universally accepted. To mention them briefly:

1. *The Ransom Theory,* which is the theory officially accepted by the Roman Catholic Church. According to this theory, Christ by his death paid a debt to the devil in order to ransom man, who was being held in hostage by the devil. Objections to this theory are that, first, it is too legalistic; secondly, it assumes a personal

devil (or source of evil) which is independent of God and with whom God must bargain; thirdly, it assumes, if there were such an independent devil, that he could be "bought off" — which seems unlikely.

2. *The Moral Satisfaction Theory* of Saint Anselm. According to this theory the debt that Christ paid by his death was not paid to the devil but was paid to God in order to satisfy his honor. Man's sin and rebelliousness against God has sullied God's honor, and before God can forgive man God's honor has to be repaired and satisfied. In the opinion of the writer this theory is an improvement over the Ransom Theory, for it avoids the impossible dualism of an independent devil. However, it is not completely satisfactory, for it still smacks of an unsavory legalism and it assumes a God, much as the pagans do, who sits off by himself and sulks until somebody "apple-polishes" him. In this theory there seems to be no place for a God "who first loved us," which is essential.

3. *The Substitutionary Theory* is a variation of the Moral Satisfaction Theory, but the emphasis is placed on sacrifice and the requirements of law and justice. In the Old Testament, sins must be atoned for by sacrifices. Man's sin, however, properly understood, is so enormous that there is nothing man can sacrifice which is great enough to atone for his sin, and consequently he must be condemned in order to fulfill the requirements of law and justice. But Christ comes to man's rescue. In going to the cross, Christ substitutes himself for man, offers a vicarious sacrifice for man, paying the price man cannot pay, and thus satisfies the requirements of law and justice. As a result it is now possible for God to be reconciled with man. The defenders of this theory rely rather heavily on the Old Testament sacrificial system, but they point out that there are New Testament passages, notably in Hebrews, which look upon Christ's work chiefly as a substitutionary sacrifice. There is some truth in all this; however, as with the previous theories this one seems too legalistic to be completely satisfactory.

4. *The Moral Influence Theory* of Abélard. According to the

first two theories, the Ransom and the Moral Satisfaction Theories, the change that Christ's act brought about was outside of men; it brought about a change either in the devil or in God. In the Substitutionary Theory man does nothing himself. These theories are therefore sometimes called "objective theories." The Moral Influence Theory is called "subjective" because according to it the change did not take place in either God or the devil (the devil is not even considered), but it takes place — at least it should — in men. Christ, by his death and example, showed men how they should live in order to be reconciled with God. His death exerts a moral influence which, when properly understood, will lead men to change their lives and be made "at one" with God. It is not surprising that this theory, which places the emphasis on man's ability to change himself, was popular in the nineteenth century and in the twentieth in so far as there was consideration of the atonement. It also has the advantage of escaping the whole legalistic bookkeeping system of debts and precise payments. However, if the position we have outlined about the fundamental nature of man as a sinner is correct, then this theory is inadequate. It misunderstands the nature of man and it woefully underestimates the selfishness and sin of man. It denies the fundamental New Testament position. "For by grace you have been saved through faith; and this is not your own doing, it is the gift of God" (Eph. 2:8).

5. *The Dramatic Theory* of Aulén. According to this theory, in Christ's death on the cross there was a real conflict and a real battle on a superhuman level. It was no play-acting, and it was not, so to speak, God playing checkers with himself. It was a real and decisive struggle between God and the power of evil, whatever that may be. In this conflict God is the major actor. He initiates the struggle ("from first to last it is the work of God himself") [45] because of his love for man. He is not paying a debt to the devil, nor to anyone else, and he is not trying simply to satisfy his own honor. Neither is he giving men an example of nobility which will lead them to change themselves. The cross represents a titanic conflict and victory — we know it was a victory because

of the resurrection. "Christ—Christus Victor—fights against and triumphs over the evil powers of the world, the 'tyrants' under which mankind is in bondage and suffering, and in him God reconciles the world to himself."[46] Thus this theory shows us "the atonement as *a movement of God to man,* and God as closely and personally engaged in the work of man's deliverance."[47]

Thus we have various theories of the atonement; perhaps no one of them is completely satisfactory, for in the atonement something happened which mere human words can never quite measure. As George Thomas has wisely put it, "It is well to make clear at the outset that the Church is committed only to the belief that Christ was crucified for the sins of men and that the cross has the power to redeem those who see in it both the love of God and his condemnation of sin." The Christian doctrine of the atonement tries to express "the conviction of generation after generation of Christians that somehow on the cross the forces of evil met the power of God in mortal combat and were decisively beaten."[48]

The importance of this combat and victory to which the atonement points will depend, as has already been implied, on our attitude and judgment concerning the fundamental nature of man. Obviously if we think of man as essentially good, and as capable, by proper education, of saving himself without any other assistance, then the doctrine of the atonement is not only useless, it is an actual hindrance in man's self-development. But we have consistently maintained in this book that man, properly understood, is fundamentally a sinner forever incapable of saving himself. In this case the atonement becomes both the most realistic and the most hopeful fact of human experience. It is realistic because the atonement takes sin with absolute seriousness. It recognizes what we have seen to be a fact: that man's sin is so serious that he cannot solve it himself. But this doctrine is also hopeful in that after recognizing the full tragedy of man's situation it claims that God himself in and through Jesus Christ has come to man's rescue and offers him a way out—forgiveness and redemption. It is because of the atonement that we know that "although we are unacceptable we are accepted."

It is impossible to elaborate here the full significance of the atonement for our daily practical living, but I hope the imaginative reader can draw his own conclusions. Words like " sin," " forgiveness," " redemption," " atonement " are cold words and almost meaningless for many moderns, but the ideas they stand for are pregnant with the stuff of living. In closing this section on the work of our Lord Jesus Christ, I would quote from the late great French Protestant and World Council leader, Pierre Maury:

" The Church must learn once again to speak of free pardon. . . . Thus, as in all great epochs of its history, the Church fulfills her responsibility only by proclaiming before all else Christ Jesus and him crucified. This is the Church's responsibility; it is also the only chance of making herself heard and believed. For outside the Church, who proclaims to modern man, tormented by his guilty conscience, God's offer of forgiveness? Who else offers this forgiveness in its reality, as the end of guilt from which modern man is trying in vain to struggle free, as an opportunity to begin life completely afresh, and to have real peace within? Who else offers their deliverance either to individuals or to nations? The world's crown of sorrows lies in the fact that no word is heard of God's forgiveness."

CHAPTER

VII

The Church

ULTIMATELY, AS WE HAVE SEEN, CHRISTIANITY MUST JUSTIFY ITSELF in the lives of individual persons, if it is to justify itself at all. It is always the individual who becomes a Christian; and his becoming a Christian is the result of his personal act of faith and commitment, which no one else can make for him. This fact, however, has led many people to assume that corporate or communal Christianity, i.e., the Church, is either of no significance or, at best, of secondary significance. Among such people the Church is looked upon as something that is *there,* so to speak; it perhaps fills a more or less important role as a moral and social stabilizer which right-minded citizens should support, but it is not essential to Christian living. (Think of the number of people, and even clergy, who say, " It is not necessary to belong to a church in order to be a good Christian.") In fact, the Church is sometimes looked upon as an obstacle to Christian living. Although honesty compels us to admit that the churches and churchmen have often failed badly, such attitudes reveal a profound misunderstanding of the role of the Church in history, in Christian life, and in doctrine. For better or for worse Christianity always has been and always will be a " Church religion "; there can be no permanent Christianity without the Church. Therefore to the question of the Church we now turn.

At the outset, in considering the Church, it is very important to keep in mind what might be called the dual nature of the Church, or the distinction between the Church (capital C) and the churches (small c). This distinction will be amplified later, but for the moment it is most important for the reader to remember that while the Church manifests itself in this world in the churches, the churches are made up of sinful people, and that consequently no particular church should ever be *completely* identified with the Church. In our discussion we shall consider first the nature of the Church, and then the relation of the Church to the churches.

1. The Nature of the Church

When we come to the question of the nature of the Church, that is, what the Church really is, or ought to be, and how it should be organized, particularly as to how it should express itself in society, we enter a very controversial area — except for Roman Catholics. The Roman Catholics have a rigid and precise doctrine of the Church. It will appear later why we believe that the Roman doctrine of the Church is heretical, but it certainly has the advantage of preciseness and definiteness which some Protestants, in their weaker moments, envy.

Protestant thought about the nature of the Church is more ambiguous. The Protestant Reformation was an attempt, and on the whole a successful one, to recapture New Testament Christianity. It was a protest against the post-Biblical accretions of the medieval Church, and an attempt to get back to the simple purity of the New Testament. Unfortunately, however, when it comes to the nature of the Church, the New Testament lacks preciseness too; more than one kind of Church life is reflected in the New Testament. Scholars still dispute concerning the nature of the New Testament Church, especially as to what it means for the contemporary Church. Consequently Protestantism reveals a wide variety of forms and opinions, ranging from the Quakers, who believe that the Church should be primarily a fellowship of those who have, or seek, the "Inner Light," to Anglo-Catholics, who believe the Church is primarily for the dispensation of saving sacraments through priests properly ordained in the "correct" apostolic succession. It is of considerable significance that the modern ecumenical movement, while seeking unity among Christian Churches and bemoaning the divisions that separate us, is at the same time emphatically declaring that it is for " unity but not uniformity," and it happily recognizes that different traditions (denominations) have an equally valid New Testament base (see I Cor. 12: 4-6).

This principle of the ecumenical movement, " unity but not uniformity," indicates that although there is a healthy diversity in Protestantism, particularly in the area of forms of church government and worship, there is also a basic unity which is far firmer than would appear from a casual and uninformed glance at the many denominations. In one way or another they all go back to the New Testament; the richness of their diversity reflects the richness of diversity in the New Testament. And the possibility of unity which is evidenced by the rapid growth of ecumenicity in our time is based on the unity of the New Testament. Without attempting anything like a minute study, and without trying to defend one form of church organization against others as being the only legitimate New Testament form, let us consider briefly the general New Testament picture of the nature of the Church.

One of the basic difficulties in trying to pin down the nature of the New Testament Church is that the Church appears to have grown like Topsy. Underneath this development Christians have always believed the Holy Spirit was at work, but externally the Church appears to have grown at random wherever Christians happened to have spread — in each locality the gospel was adapted to local conditions. There was no thought of a formal organization in the earliest years. In Acts 6: 1-6 there is an account of the appointment of seven deacons, and Paul writing to the Corinthians around A.D. 56 does say, " And God has appointed in the church first apostles, second prophets, third teachers, then workers of miracles, then healers, helpers, administrators, speakers in various kinds of tongues " (I Cor. 12: 28), but these reports are not very helpful for pin-pointing the nature of the Church. Nowhere do we find a record of a constitution for the Church; nowhere do we find a formal creed, nor a description of the organization of a local church. Paul, in a number of places, speaks of the Church as " the Body of Christ," a useful term as we shall see, but also lacking preciseness.

The chief reason why there is so little discussion of the Church is that the early Christians expected the Second Coming of Christ (technically called the Parousia) and the end of the world so soon that there was neither time nor interest for setting up or defining an institution for " the long haul." Even Paul, at least in his earlier letters, expected the end of the world shortly. It was only when later generations of Christians were forced by circumstance to recognize that the Parousia was not coming as soon as first expected that formal church organization began to appear, and that there were debates as to what should be the nature of the Church. But the process was relatively late in developing and it was long and drawn out, as any reader of Church history knows. In fact, it is part of the Protestant principle that this task is never complete; one of the errors of the Roman Catholic Church is that it has defined the Church too soon and too rigidly and thereby tried to strait-jacket the Holy Spirit.

How much this New Testament expectation of the early return of Christ goes back to our Lord himself is a very moot question. It partly depends upon how much one believes that the apocalyptic passages, especially those in Mark, ch. 13, and Matthew, chs. 24 and 25, were genuinely said by Jesus and were intended to be taken at their face value. This is one of the most controversial areas of New Testament scholarship and we cannot go into that debate here. However, it is difficult to see how the hope of the Parousia could be so strong and widespread in the New Testament Church without the original idea going back to something Jesus himself said. In any event, one of the surprising things is that Jesus said so little about the nature of the Church; in fact, some scholars question whether he ever gave any instructions for founding the Church.

In all the Gospels there are only two specific references to the Church attributed to Jesus. Both are found in Matthew. One is in

Matthew's account of Peter's confession (ch. 16: 13-20), and the other is in his account of Jesus' discussion of forgiveness (ch. 18: 15-20). The first of these is the more controversial because it contains the famous passage: " And I tell you, you are Peter, and on this rock I will build my church, and the powers of death ['gates of hell' in the King James Version] shall not prevail against it. I will give you the keys of the kingdom of heaven, and whatever you bind on earth shall be bound in heaven, and whatever you loose on earth shall be loosed in heaven " (vs. 18-19). It is on these verses that the Roman Catholic Church builds its authority, claiming that Jesus here gave the authority to " bind " and " loose " specifically to Peter, who became the first bishop of Rome (pope), from A.D. 42 to 67, and who has passed on this authority to subsequent bishops of Rome by the apostolic succession.

The Roman claim when presented dogmatically to the uninformed can be impressive, but it is also very suspect. The origin of the Church in Rome is shrouded in mystery. The earliest historical reference is that of the Roman Suetonius, who speaks, in A.D. 50, of riots in the Jewish quarter " at the instigation of one Chrestus." As the center of the Empire, it is probable that Rome had Christians numbered among the population at a fairly early date. The Acts speaks of there being " visitors from Rome, both Jews and proselytes " at the Pentecost meeting (Acts 2: 10). But Peter is not mentioned among the people to whom greetings are sent in the sixteenth chapter of Paul's letter to the Romans, nor is he among those who meet Paul when Paul arrived in Rome in A.D. 61 (Acts 28: 11-31). In fact, the earliest record of Peter's being in Rome is a letter of Clement written at the end of the first century which speaks of Peter's dying a martyr's death under Nero, but it says nothing about his having been bishop. As early as that, there were no bishops. The earliest record of Peter being the first bishop of Rome does not appear until the end of the third century.

Then there are many scholars who question whether Jesus ever really said the words as reported in Matthew. The words are not included in the parallel passages in Mark (ch. 8: 27-30) or Luke (ch. 9: 18-22); and in the only other passage that contains a direct reference to the Church (Matt. 18: 17-19) the same instructions are given to the disciples — apparently all of them. (See also John 20: 22-23, which is also said to all the disciples.) Further, it is strange, to say the least, that Jesus should give such specific instructions for the Church, recorded only in Matthew, and for the rest be so silent about such a crucial matter. The Gospels, as we know, were written relatively late — Matthew in its present form must have been written fifty or more years after Jesus' death — and each Gospel reflects the locality in which it was written. Consequently some scholars feel that these words were put into the mouth of Jesus at a later date to strengthen the authority of the Church and of the bishop of Rome.

More conservative scholarship is inclined to feel that this report in Matthew may well go back to some statement of Jesus'. The fact that John's Gospel, so different in many ways, reports the same idea in a totally different context and in slightly different words (ch. 20: 22, 23), namely, that the whole Church, or the disciples, have the power to forgive sin, strengthens this interpretation. On this basis the "rock" on which the Church is founded is not Peter, the man, but the faith he professed: "You are the Christ, the Son of the living God" (Matt. 16: 16). And any church that professes that Jesus is the Christ is the Church against which the gates of death, or hades, or hell, cannot prevail. It is certainly not limited to those which can trace a direct connection to Peter, even if that were possible, for it would eliminate even in the first century all the churches founded by Paul. Paul emphatically declared that he did not derive his authority from Peter or any man, but directly from God (Gal. 1: 1, 11).

These brief references are all that we have that may be attributed to Jesus regarding the Church and they give no real direction for the nature or organization of the Church. It would appear that Jesus, during his lifetime, did not think this an important enough issue to dwell on. Whether or not Jesus' "silence" about the formation of the Church came from his immediate expectation of the end of the world is a question no man can answer with authority. In the opinion of the writer, Jesus was not attempting to found a new church or a new religion; rather, he was primarily leading a "reform movement" within Judaism which would lead it back, or prepare it, for its true vocation for the Kingdom of God.[49] As Jesus' ministry progressed, opposition increased, and failure, as far as any large numbers were concerned, became obvious, Jesus naturally drew together an inner fellowship of those who believed in and accepted him. These he trained to carry on after his death. However, during his lifetime it is doubtful if even this inner group understood very much of what was happening; certainly there is no evidence that they considered themselves a church. But with Jesus' resurrection and the subsequent illumination of the Holy Spirit the inner group began to realize a new self-consciousness of being a unique fellowship. Under the power of this new self-consciousness the fellowship not only held together, it began to grow. This power and growth was attributed to the work of the Holy Spirit.

When one examines the sermons and preaching message (kerygma) in The Acts and also in Paul's writings, although there are variations, the central message is clear. God had acted in history, fulfilling his ancient promises in the Scriptures (Old Testament). He had sent his unique Son (Messiah, Christ) to inaugurate a new age of which the fellowship of those who accepted this is the representative. The proof of this is (1) the prophecies in the Old Testament which are seen as fulfilled in Jesus; (2) Jesus' mighty works during his lifetime; and (3), most important of all, his resurrection — in fact the resurrection is the *sine qua non* which substantiates the other proofs. While it was the business of those in the fellowship to witness to what had happened (happened both in them and in the world), outsiders were "called" or "elected"[50] by the Holy Spirit. The process by which one became a Christian and a member of the fellowship (the two are inseparable in the New Testament) cannot be pin-pointed step by step, but it included an experience of illumination in which one recognized that Jesus is the Christ, accompanied by a sense of repentance and forgiveness; Baptism, the receiving of the Holy Spirit; and finally active witness in the life of the fellowship. This participation seems to have included preaching the Word or witnessing, and regular attendance at the meeting of the fellowship (normally the first day of the week), where there were prayers, hymns, reading of the Scriptures, exposition and testimony, and celebrating the Lord's Supper, or love (agape) feasts.

When we consider this whole development certain things seem clear which may give us some clues for understanding the nature of the Church. The evidence that Jesus deliberately intended to found a Church in the usual meaning of that word is, at best, highly doubtful; but he did create a fellowship of believers in him who were held together in that fellowship by their commonly shared faith in him. That fellowship survived the shock of his death. It was given understanding in his resurrection and it was given power and direction by the Holy Spirit at Pentecost; so the fellowship grew and spread. At first, because of the immediate expectation of the Parousia, little attention was paid to organization. (The choosing of the deacons — Acts 6:1-6 — is obviously meeting an emergency.) As the hope of the Parousia dimmed and the Church spread, organizational forms just naturally and inevitably developed, but not without controversy. Nevertheless the Church that later developed was a direct continuation of the fellowship of the inner group that Jesus created during his lifetime. The external forms did change, but the latter were the direct outgrowth of the former, and in both cases it was essentially a fellowship or community of believers united by their faith that Jesus is the Christ, the Son of the Living God. This is why Paul rightly calls the Church "the Body of Christ." He recognized that the Church continues the work of Christ. Put it this way: God's ultimate revelation of salvation for men was made through Jesus Christ; that is, it was revealed to men through the body and work of a particular man. After Christ's death and resurrection that particular body disappeared as all bodies must, but the revelation of salvation was continued. Just as it was contained and "made known" in the body of Jesus as a witness to the world in his lifetime, so it is continually contained and made known in the Church as a witness to the world down through the ages "till he come."

This says something important about the Church which is not

always understood today. As the creation of Christ—or, if one prefers, as the creation of God through Christ—*the Church is something other than and different from all other social institutions.* Because the Church, seen from the outside, has sociological characteristics such as an institutional life and history, and observable interactions with society and other social phenomena, it is frequently classified as just another social institution. Of course, as we shall see in the next section, the Church has sociological manifestations, but *to try to understand the Church strictly in sociological categories is completely to misunderstand the true nature of the Church.* The Church is the creation of God—the Body of Christ—the God-given agency to carry the message of salvation to the ends of the earth and the end of the world.

From this there follow several implications about the nature of the Church. These are sometimes phrased: "The Church is One, Holy, Ecumenical, and Apostolic." The Church is *One* because Christ came to make us all one (John 17:21), and because Christ is the head of the Church into whom all parts of the Church are "knit" together (Eph. 4:15-16; also ch. 1:22 and Col. 1:18). No part or segment of the Church can disinherit any other part, or say that it has no need of it (I Cor. 12:14-16). The Church is *Holy* because it is the Body of Christ and the Creation of Christ and Christ is of God (John, chs. 10:30; 17:21) and God is holy. Therefore the Church—the fellowship of Christians—is holy. "Do you not know that you are God's temple. . . . For God's temple is holy, and that temple you are." (I Cor. 3:16-17.) The Church is *Ecumenical* in that it is catholic or universal. It is ecumenical because as Aulén says, "The act of God in Christ has universal significance and purpose,"[51] and although there are "varieties of gifts, . . . of service, . . . of working" there is the "same Spirit, . . . the same Lord, . . . the same God" (I Cor. 12:4). The term *Apostolic* is more controversial because of the special use made of "the apostolic succession" by the Roman and Anglo-Catholics. In their definitions it is something mechanical, to an outsider, even magical; it is a special power limited to the ecclesiastical hierarchy and those to whom they dispense it. The

New Testament does not support such an interpretation. Rather, the Church is apostolic in that it carries on, proclaims, and defends the gospel and the faith first given to the apostles. Wrote Paul to the Corinthians: "For I delivered to you as of first importance what I also received, that Christ died for our sins in accordance with the scriptures, that he was buried, that he was raised on the third day. . . . Whether then it was I or they [the other apostles], so we preach and so you believed." (I Cor. 15:3-4, 11.) As long as the Church proclaims this message it is apostolic, and all who witness to this faith are in the apostolic succession.

There follow from the realization that the Church is the Body of Christ at least two implications that need brief but emphatic clarification. One is that *as the Body of Christ the Church is indestructible*. We all too frequently hear well-meaning people, often clergymen, say, "What will happen to the Church?", or, "Unless the Church does so and so, it will be lost or destroyed!" Anyone making such a statement simply reveals a lack of understanding as to what the Church really is. (It may be legitimate to ask seriously, "What will happen to particular churches?"—but this is another question; see section 3 below). The Church as the Body of Christ is under the care of Christ and he has overcome the world. Nothing can happen to the Church but good. If, assuming the impossible, the Church were ever really destroyed, it would mean that Christ is not Christ and that the whole Christian faith is a delusion.

The second implication is that if the Church is the God-given agency, the Body of Christ, *it is impossible to be a Christian and not be in—actively in—the Church*. The idea expressed by many, mentioned at the beginning of this chapter, namely, that it is not necessary to be in the Church in order to be a good Christian, is impossible; anyone making such a statement reveals how far he has failed to understand, or let himself be gripped by, the Christian faith. What is really meant by persons who make such statements (and they reveal the degree to which Christianity has degenerated in our time) is that they can live ethically without being in the Church. One of the tragedies of liberalism is that it has tended to identify, in the minds of many, Christianity and ethics. In the nineteenth and early twentieth centuries there developed, for reasons that are understandable but which we cannot treat here, an emphasis on " Jesus as teacher and example." To a very large degree, being a Christian was equated with following the teachings and example of Jesus — almost always interpreted as Jesus' ethical teachings and example. However widespread, this is a serious misunderstanding of the Christian faith.

In the first place, as we made clear in our discussion of man as sinner, it is simply humanly impossible for us to live the ethical teachings of Jesus or to follow his example completely. In the second place, it is a fact only too painfully observable that many non-Christians live lives as sensitively ethical as do many Christians. Indeed, all too often the non-Christians are more ethically sensitive, especially on social issues, than lots of Christians. If Christianity is equated with ethics, it is certainly true that one can be a good Christian without being in the Church. But if what has been said so far in this book is in any sense true, Christianity is not primarily an ethic, as even a careful reading of the teachings of Jesus makes clear. Christianity *has* an ethic which is very important, and ethical living must always be important to the sincere Christian. Nevertheless, the ethic is secondary and derivative; it is not primary; it is the result, but not the cause. The primary feature of Christianity is obedience to the God revealed in Jesus Christ. On this basis the Christian must be " in Christ," and that can only mean to be in — actively in — the Church. The Church is one of the " givens " by God, and, as such, a person in becoming a Christian accepts what God has given as a demonstration of his obedience. Further, one of the requirements Christians are called upon to fulfill is that of witnessing. We cannot pursue here the full implications of witnessing, but witnessing is the only way we can demonstrate obedience. Thus, active participation in the Church and especially at stated times of worship is a witness of obedience to God and to Christ. To fail in active participation in the Church is to defy the authority of God — this no serious Christian can do.

Secondly, on a less theological and more pragmatic level, persons who say that they can be good Christians outside of the Church do not understand the full implications of what they are saying. If they are true Christians, they have received something that is of tremendous value to their lives. The only reason they have received this is that the Church has preserved it down through the ages and made it possible for them to know about it. Even at the strictly ethical level this is true; we know what the Christian ethic involves only because the Church has preserved it and made it known. Therefore, the person who tries to live the life of a Christian outside the Church is deriving values from that to which he returns nothing. Not only is this selfishly unchristian, it is actually parasitical, for a parasite by definition is something that lives off something else without returning anything. To call such a position Christian is a contradiction in terms.

2. The Sacraments

According to the New Testament the Church has just two sacraments, Baptism and the Lord's Supper. The other five so-called sacraments of the Roman Catholic Church, however ingenious they are as human inventions, do not have Biblical authority.

For many persons outside the Church, and unhappily for too many church members as well, these sacraments are baffling and are looked upon as "survivals." In my college sociology course a "survival" was defined as "a thing that was of use once, is of use no longer, but still persists." Nevertheless the sacraments are an essential part of the Church; and, in spite of all the respect and admiration we may have for groups like the Quakers which ignore them, we cannot dispense with them.

Volumes can and have been written on the sacraments. It is not our intention to go into an elaborate discussion here. Because a sacrament by definition is "an outward and visible sign of an inner and spiritual grace" there will always be something illusive and mysterious about the sacraments. No human being can completely and satisfactorily explain them. In the opinion of the writer the simplest way to understand and accept the sacraments is to recognize that they are part of the " givens " of the Church and of the Christian Faith. They are ordained of God as essential parts of the Church which he also ordained, and they should be accepted as such. In taking them, we witness to God, to ourselves and to others, that we have submitted to what God has ordained and are obedient to his commands. It is not necessary that we know or can explain all the " whys and wherefores " (just as we cannot explain all the " whys and wherefores " of a great many of God's actions). It is only necessary that we accept them as essential parts of our obedience to God. When seriously accepted on this basis they do become amazing means of grace, as " ten thousand times ten thousand " down through the ages can testify, even though they could not explain what happened or how.

Beyond this, Baptism is from the earliest days an essential " given " of the Church as a precondition for membership. Sociologically speaking, Baptism has an affinity with initiation rites which are virtually universal. Even baptism by water is not in itself uniquely Christian, for John the Baptist, as well as other groups, practiced water baptism. The significant fact about Christian Baptism is not that it employed a rather widespread form; but rather, that for faith, and when done in obedience, it became an essential " given " of the life of the Christian and of the life of the Church. Various other additional interpretations of Baptism can and have been made. Since, as we have seen, all men are sinners, Baptism has been looked upon as washing away one's original or natural sin; or, since becoming a Christian means becoming a " new creation " (Gal. 6:15), Baptism symbolizes the necessary purification before one can be a " new creation," eligible for the membership in the society of new beings — the Church. Since this becoming a new creation also involves the death of what we were before, Baptism (and the symbolism of this is more real in total immersion) is a process of dying and being reborn. " Do you not know that all of us who have been baptized into Christ Jesus were baptized into his death? We were buried therefore with him by baptism into death, so that as Christ was raised from the dead by the glory of the Father, we too might walk in newness of life." (Rom. 6:3-4.) No one of these interpretations excludes the others, and behind all of them is the act of obedience to what God has ordained which, when made, is a means of grace.

The question of infant Baptism is more debatable. Infant Baptism does not seem to have been practiced in the New Testament Church and those who defend the practice (and that includes much the largest number of churches) do not defend it as being literally Scriptural. Some churches, chiefly those in the Anabaptist tradition, have insisted, both on New Testament and on pragmatic grounds, that since Baptism is the way into the new life and the Church it cannot be performed except for a person who has reached the age of discretion and can make a responsible decision. A good case can be made for this position. At the same time Baptism means being taken into a community, a fellowship in which all have Christian responsibility for each other. It was probably inevitable that Christian parents wanted their children to grow up in the care of and as the responsibility of the fellowship — that is, the Church — and so infant Baptism developed at a very early date.[52] Among the large number of Protestant Churches that practice infant Baptism it is not considered that the rite makes the infant a full member of the Church (that remains a decision for one who has reached the age of discretion); it only provisionally brings the infant into the care of the Household of Faith.

The issue of infant versus adult Baptism does not seem to me a very important one as long as infant Baptism is not interpreted as a mechanical and magical device to prevent some babies from going to hell. And the issue of whether one is immersed or sprinkled seems even less important. What is important is that we recognize this sacrament as one of the "givens" that God has ordained as a means of grace.

Perhaps the most tragic aspect of the human life of the Church, which is the illustration par excellence of our human finiteness and sin, is the fact that that which was given to unite us — the sacrament of the Lord's Supper, or Holy Communion — is the one practice which more than anything else divides us. Not only are Protestants and Roman Catholics irreconcilably divided, but within the Protestant tradition there are divisions as to meanings and methods so passionately held that we are confronted at great ecumenical conferences with the necessity of having several different Communion services. To deal with an analysis of why this is so would take us too far afield, although what was said in Chapter IV, on man, and what will be said in the section that follows, "The Church and the Churches," should give some understanding to the discerning reader. Needless to say, in any area as controversial as this it is impossible that any one man can write what will be acceptable to all.

In general there have been three main traditions of the sacrament of Communion, at least in Western Christendom. There is the Roman Catholic theory of "transubstantiation," in which it is believed that Jesus meant literally his physical body and blood when he said: "This is my body. . . . This is my blood." (To an outsider this makes no more sense than saying that when Jesus said, "I am the door," he meant that he was a slab of wood with hinges and a handle.) According to this theory, the bread and wine actually become the body and blood of Christ by a physical miracle although remaining under the "accidents" of bread and wine. The power to perform this miracle is the special power of priests, properly ordained; but when they use it, it works inevitably and automatically. The recipient literally eats God and thereby takes God into his system.

The Protestant Reformers rejected the Roman doctrine as being too magical, mechanical, and carnal, along with other practices felt to be abuses that had grown up in the Roman Mass. Writes J. B. Phillips: "It is worth noting in passing that the very word 'hocus-pocus' is a corruption of part of the consecration words of the Latin Mass, '*hoc est enim corpus meum*.' It [the Protestant Reformation] was a revolt against the whole magical bag of tricks with which the Roman Catholic Church had stifled the sublime simplicity of New Testament Christianity." [53] Luther developed a position known as "consubstantiation." He rejected the physical miracle of the Roman Church as being too magical and mechanical, but he wished to affirm that Christ was truly present in the Communion. Luther developed his doctrine against Zwingli, who interpreted the Communion primarily as a memorial. In the Lutheran position the bread and the wine are symbols, but they are symbols of a *real* presence of Christ. Zwingli, who most influenced the Free Church tradition, placed the emphasis upon our Lord's words: "Do this in remembrance of me." However, Zwingli meant far more by a memorial than many of his later followers realized.

"He did not say that one partakes of the elements simply in memory of Jesus whom one thinks of as significant in some way or another. He meant that through this act, instituted in the New Testament, the believer is graphically reminded of and participates in the total drama of God's redeeming activity in Christ. . . . This act is a visible sign in which is telescoped the total gospel in a way words could not convey. The remembrance is a dramatic presentation of the whole of that which is at the basis of faith."[54]

Calvin's position was actually much nearer Luther's. He insisted on the real presence of Christ, although "unlike Luther, he did not spell it out in a metaphysical way."[55]

Unfortunately, besides these theological or metaphysical differences there are also what might be called practical differences in administration, such as: who has the authority to conduct the Communion and make it valid, and in what form it should be presented. These administrative differences, of course, have their theological bases, but at the working level they present strongly held administrative difficulties: for instance, whether one cup from which all drink should be used or whether many cups (distributed); more important, who can properly administer the Communion. In the more sacramental and liturgical churches such as the Anglican only the priest properly ordained in the proper apostolic succession can make the ministering valid. In some of the Free Churches where the doctrine of the "priesthood of all believers" is emphasized (such as the Congregational), laymen, or at least deacons, can legitimately perform the service. All too often the right way is assumed to be the way the particular church or denomination uses, other methods being considered invalid.

These divisions at the heart of the Christian enterprise are discouraging. They are more than discouraging; they are judgments upon our human sin, finiteness, and arrogance. But at the same time they cannot be dismissed lightly. It is very important to remember that these divisions arise because the churches take this sacrament so seriously. It is a sacrament given and instituted by Christ. Therefore, it is not something for men to tamper with, but to accept as given. We frequently hear people say: " Why not all get together and agree on one form and be done with it? We are all Christians, are we not? " Such statements are usually made by persons who interpret Christianity primarily as an ethic and who have never delved seriously into the question of the sacrament of the Last Supper. Our differences arise from the fact that being human we interpret what is given variously, but these differences point also to a unity in recognizing the absolute importance of the sacrament as a given. Happily, although there is still a long way to go, there appears to be arising within the ecumenical movement a new appreciation of the validity of forms other than one's own.

As indicated above, probably no one, certainly not the writer, can resolve all these theological and administrative differences to the satisfaction of everyone. The writer stands in the Free Church tradition for which he believes there is a solid New Testament base. Therefore, the bread and the wine are interpreted symbolically with the understanding that the ultimates of life can be expressed only in symbols. There is a mystery here which can never be completely and rationally explained. Like Christ himself the sacrament of the Lord's Supper is the new wine which bursts all the wineskins in which men try to confine it. *A miracle does take place at the Communion, but it takes place in the believer's heart.* Beyond this the best way to cut the Gordian knot of differences about this sacrament is to recognize the principle stated at the beginning of this section and already applied to Baptism.

The Last Supper is a sacrament given by God through Christ. We who are in Christ must accept it (in whatever form) as such, as a sign of our obedience and of our being in Christ. When we do so, grace follows.

3. The Church and the Churches

At the beginning of this chapter we called attention briefly to what we termed "the dual nature of the Church" and made a distinction between the Church (capital C) and the churches (small c). In the previous sections we have confined our discussion largely to the nature of the Church. The Church described, however, even to the most casual reader, will seem a far cry from the Second Church on Tenth and Main Streets. It is most important to understand why this discrepancy exists and what is the relation between the Church and the churches.

The Church exists perfectly only in the Kingdom of God. The Church manifests itself on earth in the human situation in two ways. One is the "invisible Church," the fellowship of all true believers who are sincerely trying to live the Christian life as God gives them grace. No one can say who these people are, how many they are, or that they are all in some particular church. Certainly they are fewer in number than the membership on our church rolls indicates. Conceivably some might not be in any church, although that would be a very rare case and presumably would not continue for long (as, for instance, a man converted in some inaccessible area where no formal church existed). This Church continues to exist by the grace of God down through the ages. This is the Church manifested on earth which Paul had in mind when he wrote: "We are afflicted in every way, but not crushed; perplexed, but not driven to despair; persecuted, but not forsaken; struck down, but not destroyed" (II Cor. 4:8-9).

Secondly, the Church manifests itself in particular churches and denominations. Unfortunately these particular churches are all most people ever see. As the senior demon, Screwtape, wrote to his junior tempter, Wormwood:

"I do not mean the Church as we see her spread out through all time and space and rooted in eternity, terrible as an army with banners. . . . But fortunately it is quite invisible to these humans. All your patient sees is the half-finished sham Gothic erection on the new building estate." [56]

Most people see only an institution with observable sociological characteristics, some of which are not inspiring. This is an inevitable limitation of human finiteness and of this world. It is of considerable significance that in the vision of the Seer of Revelation, in his description of the Holy City, and the New Jerusalem in the age to come, there is no mention of a church (Rev., chs. 21 to 22:5), for there will be no need for one. The institutional church is a condition of this world. It is an evidence of God's love and grace granted us for our earthly pilgrimage. But in this world the Church is necessary, and it is inevitable that in its manifestations in this world it became institutionalized. It is simply impossible to perpetuate any idea very far or very long in history without embodying it in an institution whose business it is to preserve, extend, and perpetuate the idea. The Church in its earthly life cannot escape this law of human existence; neither does it escape entirely what seems to be a corollary law of all institutions, namely, that they become rigid and stereotyped, and lose to a greater or lesser degree the pristine glory of the original idea. Consequently the churches are always considerably less than their ideal of what they should be and claim to be. All churches are made up of people like you and me, finite, sinful people — people whose glands get out of order, who have had bad conditioning, and who, being finite, have partial perspectives which they tend to absolutize. As we have tried to emphasize before, the church people are not better than other people; in fact, the Church is not for "good people" — it is for people who know they are not good enough and want God's forgiveness and grace to carry on and try to do better.

It is very important that we constantly keep in mind this inevitable human element of the churches; if we do, it will help us understand why the churches are as they are, and it may make us a little more charitable in our judgments. It always has been possible, and always will be, to point to any one of the Christian virtues and show how woefully short the churches and churchmen have fallen. In fact, it is not altogether unfair to say that, at one time or another, the churches have committed about every crime there is; and if their sins of commission are bad, their sins of omission are even worse! All this is true, for the Church always manifests itself in churches made up of people who are only people. It is very easy for the superficial to become supercritical of the churches. No other institution in society is judged as critically as are the churches. This is probably as it should be, for the Church claims to be the earthly representative of the Kingdom of God. Nevertheless, to rearrange slightly the teaching of our Lord: before we see the log in the churches' eye we, at least, ought to recognize some of the specks in our own eyes. The churches are the way they are because we are the kinds of people we are.

It is truly amazing, and we often forget it, that in spite of their failures the churches continue to persist and to survive. No other human institution has failed so often as the Church and still survived. It has adjusted to one culture after another, and as A. J. Toynbee points out it is the only institution that survives the breakdowns of civilization.[57] This cannot be adequately explained on any rational sociological basis; it can be explained only on the assumption that, for all their humanness, the churches are manifestations of a divine society under the care of the God revealed in our Lord Jesus Christ. Consequently the churches must be thought of in dual terms — from two angles at once. *On the one hand the churches are representative of the divine society, the God-given Church which is the Body of Christ, and as such indestructible; on the other hand they are always human institutions made up of people who fail.* Actually the human is always corrupting the divine and the divine is always correcting, sometimes by hard judgment, the human.

One exception to this general statement needs to be made. Not all churches or segments of the Church are always true representatives of the Church. Sometimes particular churches, or sections of the Church, deviate so far from their calling that they can only receive a judgment that wipes them more or less out. The best interpretation of the Protestant Reformation is that it was the judgment of God on a corrupt Roman Catholic Church; in like manner the Russian Revolution was the judgment of God on a corrupt Russian Orthodox Church. One might venture the prediction that unless the Protestant Churches do better than they have on race relations they too may feel the judgment of God. Sections of the Church can and have been wiped out. Then, too, at times, the churches are purged through persecution and driven underground. All this does not negate the general principle: the Church is the Body of Christ marching down through the ages which manifests itself in the churches. The churches are constantly failing because they are made up of people, but they are also constantly being redeemed in spite of their failures because they are also the Body of Christ.

Such an understanding of the nature of the Church and its manifestations on earth should make clearer why we have churches (denominations). There are many who seem to think that denominationalism is the curse of the Church. There is, of course, some truth in this, especially when denominationalism runs rampant, becomes self-righteously exclusive, and gets out of hand. However, it does not follow that it is necessarily the curse of the Church just because denominationalism sometimes goes too far. Human nature being what it is, we see things in different ways, and we tend to associate with people who feel the way we do. The Church manifests itself in many different environments and has in it all kinds of people with different conditioning and thought patterns. It is ridiculous to assume that all these people are going to worship God through the same ritual or church government, or that they will all always emphasize the same things as being most important.

This is no new phenomenon. Denominationalism, although the word is more recent, is as old as the Church. The ancient Church contained wide varieties. Indeed, courses in Church history are largely courses in the fights, differences, reconciliations, and further splits of the Church. This goes back even to the New Testament where Paul fought "the Jerusalem crowd" over the issue of taking Gentiles into the Church. New Testament scholars speak of the "Jerusalem tradition" and the "Galilean tradition" as being quite distinct, and Paul scolds the Corinthian Church for having divisive parties within it (I Cor. 1: 10-13). It was only when the Roman Church (in Western Christianity) [58] in the later Middle Ages tried to strait-jacket both the response of Christians and the work of the Holy Spirit that Protestant denominationalism arose as a necessary protest. Denominationalism should be kept under control; that is, no denomination should ever be allowed to claim exclusive priority on the grace of God, for that limits the freedom of the Holy Spirit which is both impossible and blasphemous. Beyond that, however, denominationalism, instead of being considered the curse of the Church, should be looked upon as a sign of the grace and love of God coming to men of differing temperaments and needs and meeting them where they are.

One last thing needs to be said. As far as our practical life in this world is concerned, except for the rare exception noted above, the only way you and I can be in the Church is to be in one of the churches that is seriously trying to make itself as true a representative of the Church as it can. There is no other way you and I can be in the Church, for the Church does not exist in a vacuum; existentially it exists only in the churches. If the Church is the God-given Body of Christ, as we have maintained, and if it manifests itself existentially only in the churches, then the Christian has no alternative, in demonstrating his obedience and in living his faith, than that he be actively working in some Christian church.

CHAPTER

VIII

The Kingdom of God

As even the most casually informed are aware, the idea of a Kingdom of God (or Heaven) is a fundamental idea of the Bible. In some ways it has been one of the most persistently accepted of the Biblical ideas. In the nineteenth and early twentieth centuries when one Biblical position after another was being given up under the attacks of science, evolution, and of Biblical criticism, the idea of the Kingdom of God in a modified and often secularized form not only survived; if anything, it gained ground. Encouraged especially by the theory of evolution which was rather too easily assumed to mean that change inevitably included spiritual progress, the Kingdom of God was preached from thousands of pulpits as the goal of man's endeavors toward which we are all evolving. Although among the pious it was still called the Kingdom of God and in some vague way God had something to do with it, it was to be realized largely through men's effort. The faithful were exhorted to build the Kingdom of God on earth; and it was assumed that this was perfectly possible, in fact, almost inevitable.

The events of the twentieth century, however, have brought about a sobering re-evaluation. The spectacle of two world wars, man's obvious inhumanity to man, particularly as revealed in torture chambers and mass liquidations, the threat of atomic self-destruction, and so forth, have profoundly affected our thinking. When all is going well we do not usually question our assumptions, but when catastrophe, or the serious threat of it, comes we are forced to re-examine them. It is therefore not surprising that in the last twenty-five years there has been a rash of books dealing with the questions of the meaning and direction of history.

We have no intention of making an exhaustive survey of philosophies of history, but it is impossible to discuss the Biblical concept of the Kingdom of God intelligently without taking some brief cognizance of this question, because the idea of the Kingdom of God is part of the Biblical philosophy of history. And the Bible has a philosophy of history because the question of the meaning of history is a basic question for the meaning of human existence. Most people today, even the most educated people, are not particularly conscious of being interested in a philosophy of history; nevertheless, everyone is or ought to be, since the meaning of human existence and the meaning of history are inextricably bound together. All of us live in history and are shaped by it. If history has no meaning, neither can human life be said to have any meaning, except on a " catch as catch can " and " devil take the hindermost " basis. Biblical Christianity affirms that history and human life have meaning, a meaning which they receive from the Kingdom of God. Therefore Christianity has a very definite philosophy of history. Before, however, going on to the Christian philosophy of history as expressed in the idea of the Kingdom of God it will be necessary to make a few brief observations about the general field.

1. Various Philosophies of History

In an oversimplified way all philosophies of history can be reduced to one of three general categories: (*a*) the philosophy that it is impossible to give a coherent meaning to history; (*b*) the idea that history is static, or, if going anywhere, traveling round in cycles; (*c*) the idea that history is developing or progressing in some direction. (A fourth philosophy of history might be the theory of human degeneration, where man's " Golden Age " is put in the past as was held by Homer and Hesiod and to some extent by Rousseau. But it is not a very live option today.) Let us consider the three in the order given.

One of the first problems into which we run is the assertion that it is impossible to have a philosophy of history. First of all, it is claimed that history is too multitudinous, various, and complex for anyone to discover any persistent pattern. There are just too many facts—far more than any one person can know, much less comprehend and organize meaningfully. Secondly, as we have seen, a fact is only a fact and it is without meaning until it is interpreted by someone. The interpreter is always a product of his own age and culture, and consequently no matter how objective he tries to be his interpretation of the fact will be colored by his own conscious or subconscious prejudices. Therefore, a philosophy of history may tell us a lot about the philosopher who holds it, but it does not necessarily tell us much of anything about history or its meaning. Finally, there are always at least two and usually more interpretations in the process of giving meaning to any historical fact. There are the subjective interpretations made by the person or persons who first recorded it, and then there is the modern historian's interpretation of the original interpretation. On a strictly scientific proof basis it is impossible to prove that anything in history actually happened the way it is reported to have happened. All that we can logically say is that so-and-so reports that such-and-such happened in such-and-such a way. On this basis a philosophy of history is impossible; it is only the product of the prejudices, fears, and wish thinking of the philosophers who think it up.

Now on the assumption that the naturalistic, scientific rational-empirical method is the only avenue to truth, there is considerable to be said for this position, at least theoretically. Strictly speaking, it is impossible to prove any fact of history. In a strictly scientific sense it is impossible to prove that there was a man named Karl Marx who wrote as he is reported to have written. But for all practical human purposes this is a theoretical *reductio ad absurdum*. For all practical human purposes we know that Karl Marx lived, wrote as he did, and, as a result, the world we live in is vastly different from what it would have been. If Karl Marx and his work are unprovable illusions, they are the kind of illusions that the stuff of life is made of. If they are not existentially real facts, then not only is it impossible to have a philosophy of history, it is also impossible to say anything about life except that we live—or perhaps more accurately: "I live and others appear to live." This is, of course, driving the point to an absurd conclusion, but there are those who defend this view, at least theoretically. They live in an academic ivory tower.

In practice, of course, human nature is such that it cannot stand meaninglessness for long. As Dr. Tillich has pointed out, men can be cynical and despairing about many things but no man can continue to be cynical and despairing about everything.[59] In a reported conversation, the poet W. H. Auden was affirming this same position and insisting that every man had to find some meaning in something. He was asked about Sartre, the French existentialist, then at the height of his gospel of the meaninglessness of everything. Auden replied that Sartre found meaning in the importance he attributed to his own writings. Apparently, however, this did not satisfy Sartre for long, as he has since espoused communism! Perhaps more significant for Americans is Morris Cohen. In his *The Meaning of Human History* he rigorously attacks the idea that there can be any one legitimate philosophy of history, but in the last chapter he ends by saying that we can learn ethical lessons from history which will help us meet our problems better and build more wisely for the future. This seems to me to be in reality a doctrine of progress, but at any rate it indicates that Dr. Cohen was unable to accept the full implications of his own position. Finally, it should be pointed out that the very denial that there is any discoverable meaning in history is in itself a kind of backhanded philosophy of history. It is an attempt to understand and therefore put meaning (although of a very despairing sort) into history.

The cyclical view of history—the idea that history is moving in great repetitive cycles has its origin among the Greeks. The Pythagoreans, Plato, and Aristotle, in one way and another, believed that history moved in great cycles. A similar view was held by Virgil and Marcus Aurelius. In modern times Oswald Spengler is perhaps the best-known advocate of this view. In his *Decline of the West,* Spengler held that civilizations had a life cycle similar to man and passed through stages of infancy, growing up, adult vigor, senility, and death.

It is of course an observable fact of history that civilizations have emerged and later died to be followed by other civilizations. This, as well as other facts of life, such as the recurrence of the seasons, have led many to see a basic rhythmical movement in history. Nevertheless the cyclical interpretation of history does not necessarily follow. Cohen severely criticizes Spengler's thesis as being an artificial and "very farfetched" analogy, and points out that "no two known civilizations have gone through the supposed cycle the same way." [60] A. J. Toynbee has an even more documented criticism of Spengler, showing the fallacy of the analogy between civilization and the lives of men, and he significantly remarks, "One of the perennial infirmities of human beings is to ascribe their own failure to the operation of forces which are entirely beyond their control." [61] Toynbee further painstakingly criticizes the various theories historians have put forward to show that civilizations die of necessity, and concludes: "The dead civilizations are not 'dead by fate'; and therefore the living civilizations are not doomed inexorably in advance." [62] In spite of the obvious recurrence, growth, and degeneration which we observe in the world and in history, a thoroughgoing cyclical interpretation of history does not stand up.

At least we who are Christians cannot accept the cyclical interpretation. According to our faith God created the world and human life in it "good" (Gen., ch. 1), and he will bring it to a "good conclusion" (Jer. 31:31-34; Rev., chs. 21 to 22:5). If God is to bring history to a "good conclusion," he must of necessity be in control of the process, and a major theme of the Bible is that God is the Lord of history and continually acting in history. We Christians being finite creatures do not always understand all of God's actions, but we understand enough to affirm against all comers that the end will be good (Isa. 55:6-11; Rom. 8:18-25;

I John 3:2). We call this conclusion the Kingdom of God (or Heaven). Such an interpretation obviously implies some sort of development and ongoingness, and equally obviously it precludes meaningless and cyclical philosophies, and the idea of degeneration as well.

The idea then that history is developing — going somewhere — toward a "good conclusion" is basically Biblical and is found only among those cultures which have been informed by the Bible: Judaism, Mohammedanism, and Christianity. The one exception to this is Zoroastrianism, which also sees history as developing (although through cycles) and as the scene of a titanic struggle between the forces of good and the forces of evil. For the interested student there are many striking parallels between Zoroastrianism and Biblical thought, but Zoroastrianism lacks the dynamic freedom we find in the Bible. It is completely mechanical. History is fated to move through four cycles of three thousand years to a dramatic conclusion.

The idea of progress, which is probably the most widely held philosophy of history today, at least in Western and communist countries, is really a secularized corruption of the Biblical position. The idea of progress is a relatively new idea. Nowhere in the ancient world do we find the idea that the world was becoming better and better, or that man by his own efforts could create a perfect or even a better world.[63] As we shall see, the Bible does hold out the hope of a Messianic reign, or the Kingdom of God, toward which all history moves, but this state is always something God will give in his own good time and never a state which man can progressively create. Throughout the Middle Ages it was simply assumed that the world was more or less static and awaiting the Final Judgment and consummation. It was not until the Renaissance, with its new emphasis on man and his creative possibilities as a reasoning being, that there began to be the idea that history was progressing and the world might become better. The first real suggestion of what might be called a philosophy of progress was made by Joachim de Floris in the twelfth century. Joachim had the idea that all of history could be understood in terms of three ages: the age of the Father (from Creation to the time of Christ), the age of the Son (from the time of Christ to Joachim's time), and the age of the Holy Spirit (a glorious new age which was just dawning).

It is not our purpose to trace out this whole development, but it is interesting to note that the idea of progress was originally cast in a religious frame, as in Joachim's case, and God was given a central place in guiding the process. As time went on, however, God was given a less and less significant role, and man and man's activity became central. For vast multitudes, especially among the "enlightened," the idea of progress became increasingly secularized. C. L. Becker has shown in his *The Heavenly City of the Eighteenth Century Philosophers* how the Heavenly City "whose builder and maker is God" was transformed into an Earthly City whose builder and maker would be man. The developments in science and especially the theory of evolution in the nineteenth century and continuing into the early years of the present century gave impetus to the idea of progress and utopianism. It permeated the thinking of the religious as well as of the secular. The religious still made reference to God and they talked about building the Kingdom of God, but it was man who would build it. Except that they used different language both the religious and the secular were saying the same thing. This general attitude became so pervasive that it was taken for granted by almost everyone.

Events of the last fifty years have shaken our confidence in the inevitability of progress and in man's and history's capacity to redeem themselves. It is of more than passing significance that the three most popular utopian novels since World War I are Huxley's *Brave New World,* Orwell's *1984,* and Hilton's *Lost Horizon.* The first two are terrifying and the third is pure escapism — quite a shift from earlier optimism of, say, H. G. Wells. Man's reason and technique, good and important as they are, do not seem good enough to solve the problems erected by man's sin.

The recent historical events which have turned out so sadly different from what was expected fifty or seventy-five years ago have at least opened the door to a re-examination of the meaning of history. On such a re-examination it may be found that the Biblical Christian philosophy of history is far more cogent and realistic than previously thought.

2. The Development of the Kingdom of God Idea in the Bible

According to the gospels of Matthew and Mark, Jesus began his ministry on the theme, "Repent, for the kingdom of God [or heaven] is at hand" (Mark 1:15; Matt. 4:17). Jesus, however, was not preaching a brand-new idea. He really began on the same note as John the Baptist (Matt. 3:1-2; Luke 3:1-6). Neither was John developing a new idea. Both John and Jesus were building on a very widely held common expectation; and one of the reasons why they were relatively quickly liquidated was that there had been so many messianic movements and "Messiahs," all of which were ruthlessly put down, that the religious and civil authorities were afraid of another uprising.

The idea of the Kingdom of God, or the Messianic Hope, or the Day of the Lord, has its origin in Jewish antiquity. It first began to be more or less precisely defined by the eighth century B.C. prophets. The earliest of these, Amos, spoke of it as "the day of the Lord," and one of the things the optimistic preachers of progress have bypassed is that Amos spoke of it not as fulfillment of man's dreams but as judgment and doom. "Woe to you who desire the day of the Lord! Why would you have the day of the Lord? It is darkness, and not light. . . . Is not the day of the Lord darkness, and not light, and gloom with no brightness in it?" (Amos 5:18, 20.) But Amos could only speak of the "day of the Lord" as he did because there was already a widespread belief in the idea. The contemporary accepted idea was that on "the day of the Lord" God would intervene in history and bring peace, prosperity, and the righting of injustice to the Jewish people. Amos was merely trying to correct this idea by saying that it would be judgment rather than fulfillment.

The origin of the concept of the Kingdom of God (by whatever terms it may be called) in the Bible is obscure. It might be said to begin with Moses and the exodus when the Hebrews left Egypt to search for the "Promised Land"—"land flowing with milk and honey" (Ex. 3:8, etc.). Perhaps the origin should be pushed back farther, to the call of Abram when, "Now the Lord said to Abram, 'Go from your country and your kindred and your father's house to the land that I will show you. And I will make of you a great nation, and I will bless you, and make your name great, so that you will be a blessing . . . and by you all the families of the earth will bless themselves'" (Gen. 12:1-3). Indeed it can be argued that the idea of the ultimate establishment of a Kingdom of God is implicit in creation itself. Man is made "in the image of God" (Gen. 1:27), and although man later "sins" and "falls" (Gen., ch. 3), man did not ask to be born and therefore God as his creator has a responsibility to save him. This seems to be the meaning of Paul's argument that Christ is the "Second Adam" (see Rom., ch. 5; also I Cor. 15:45).

If it is claimed that these Old Testament stories are legends and examples of "writing back," expressing more of what the later Hebrews thought was the situation rather than the actual facts, it is still true that at a very early stage the Hebrews were deeply conscious of God's operation in history and of their peculiar relationship to him (Deut. 7:6, 7). Somehow God had chosen them and he would see that they reached fulfillment. Martin Buber claims that the highly developed concept of transcendent majesty in Isa. 45:5-10 is no different from the idea implied in the giving of the Ten Commandments (Deut. 5:6-7): "Nothing has been added or subtracted, an unconditioned character implicit at first now expresses itself explicitly."[64] This is one of the unique things about the Bible which makes it different from other histories. The Bible claims that history and especially the history of the Jews cannot be explained completely in terms of mere sociological data; it can be explained only in terms of God's special action which included his trustworthiness to redeem his promises to save his people.

Whatever the origin of the Kingdom of God idea, it was the great literary prophets who made it explicit in terms of the Messianic Hope. The Messianic Hope was a revelation to the prophets when they compared the promises of God with the realities of the historical situation. The "Promised Land," the Land of Canaan, proved not to be flowing with milk and honey in any utopian sense, but rather was full of other tribes who fought desperately to keep what they had. And even if the great King David vanquished Israel's enemies and established a goodly kingdom he had to contend with rebellions to the end of his days. After his son Solomon, the Kingdom was split and the two Kingdoms, although having ups and downs, were both eventually destroyed (Israel in 721 B.C. and Judah in 586 B.C.). In addition to this dramatic failure of the political hopes of the Hebrews there never was any remotely complete establishment of justice within the nation. The rich continued to "join house to house," and "add field to field, until there is no more room" (Isa. 5:8). "They sell the righteous for silver, and the needy for a pair of shoes — . . . and turn aside the way of the afflicted." (Amos 2:6-7). Faced with these hard realities, the prophets, in a way that can only be called revelation, recognized that men are too sinful either to establish a perfect society or to fulfill their own highest hopes. Consequently they proclaimed that since man could not save himself God would intervene and send a savior, a messiah, who as God's Anointed would condemn the evil, redeem the good, and do what man could not do. Although it was Hosea who first held out hope that, after due punishments and purification for sin, there would be forgiveness and redemption (Hos. 2:21-23; 3:4-5), it was Isaiah who first spoke of a coming messiah, an individual sent from God who would do what men could not do (Isa. 9:2-7; 11:1-5).

Actually, that the Messianic Age would be inaugurated by a messiah is not a consistent theme in the Old Testament. Sometimes it is to be inaugurated by a messiah and sometimes it is merely to be a new age of peace and justice somehow to be inaugurated by God (see Isa. 2:1-4; Jer. 31:31-34; Ezek., ch. 37; Hab. 2:1-4). But in either case, and this is what is important for an understanding of the Kingdom of God idea in the Bible, men never create it — they are too corrupt; it is always something God will do. "The zeal of the Lord of hosts will do this." (Isa. 9:7.)

Both of these strands of thought were current in the Palestinian world of Jesus; and the expectation of Messianic Age, or Kingdom of God, soon to be brought about, either with or without a messiah, was a major expectation of the average religious Jew. Most Jews thought of it in both universal and highly nationalistic terms. It was to be a new age for all people, but the Jews were to be the dominant race and Jerusalem was to be the capital. In so far as it was believed to be inaugurated by a messiah, he would be a political-military hero who would overthrow Rome. Jesus had to continue to fight this interpretation, and he interpreted his own role in terms of the Suffering Servant (Isa., ch. 53). He never really succeded in making this clear even to his most intimate disciples until after his death and resurrection. At any rate, Jesus' teaching about the Kingdom was based upon commonly accepted ideas which had a long history, but according to our records he combined, discarded, and reinterpreted to suit his purposes.

3. Jesus' Teaching on the Kingdom

During the Evanston Conference of the World Council of Churches in 1954 there was a great deal of publicity given to what was purported to be the major debate: namely, over whether the Kingdom was something that is in some sense here now, or whether it is something that comes only at the end of history and, for the present, all that Christians can do is sit around and wait for it. The writer was not present at that conference but understands that because it was "good newspaper copy" the issue was made far more of in the press than at the conference. Nevertheless the issue of the present Kingdom versus the future Kingdom is as old as Christianity and goes back to Jesus' own teachings on the subject.

When we examine carefully Jesus' thought about the Kingdom three major strands stand out. At first glance they appear to be more or less in conflict. They are: (*a*) The Kingdom as coming with judgment, suddenly and catastrophically at the end of history. (*b*) The Kingdom as coming gradually by a slow process of growth. (*c*) The Kingdom as already here. Let us examine briefly each of these three and then see how they fit together.

(*a*) *The Kingdom is coming with judgment, suddenly and catastrophically at the end of history*. The primary passages where these predictions are found are in what is known as the Little Apocalypse (Matt., chs. 24 to 25 and Mark, ch. 13. See also Luke 21:5-36). In these passages Jesus foretells the coming judgment and the end of the world in vividly catastrophic and apocalyptic [65] terms. There has been a great deal of debate among Biblical scholars as to just how genuinely these passages belong to Jesus. Some claim that they are central to the teaching of Jesus; others claim that they are not part of his original thought but rather were put into his mouth later when apocalyptic thinking dominated at least part of the Church's thought. Into the intricacies of this debate we cannot enter, but the truth is probably somewhere between the two extremes. It is certainly true that the New Testament, including the Gospels, is a product of the Early Church, and it is certainly true that apocalypticism, or "futuristic eschatology" as it is sometimes called, dominated much of the Church's thinking in the latter part of the first century. It is not at all impossible that some of these sayings attributed to Jesus were more or less unconsciously attributed to him. On the other hand, although the Early Church writers may have embroidered they did not completely invent. If the New Testament is the product of the Early Church, the Early Church, desperately anxious to be true to its Lord, preserved and built upon a solid core of what Jesus actually must have taught. It is impossible to eliminate all of Jesus' teachings about the coming judgment and end of the world. As we have seen, his message began on the note, "Repent, for the kingdom of God is at hand," and this note is basic to his whole message. It should be remembered that apocalyptic thinking was pretty much standard in the Palestine of Jesus' day and it is inevitable that he would teach in terms of the thought pattern of his day. Further, as will appear below shortly, the idea of an end to history is absolutely essential to any adequate philosophy of history. Even if the more violent passages are eliminated, it is clear that Jesus taught that the Kingdom was coming with judgment, suddenly and catastrophically at the end of history.

(*b*) *The Kingdom is coming gradually as a process of slow growth.* This teaching about the Kingdom seems to stand somewhat in contrast to the previous emphasis, although it too looks to the future for final fulfillment. The teachings on " gradualism " are best illustrated by such parables as that of the sower (Matt. 13: 1-9, 18-23; Mark 4: 1-9, 14-20; Luke 8: 4-8, 11-15), the mustard seed (Matt. 13: 31-32; Mark 4: 30-32; Luke 13: 18-19), and the parable of the leaven (Matt. 13: 33; Luke 13: 20-21). It was these teachings of Jesus that were seized upon by those who rather uncritically accepted evolution as proof of automatic progress and emphasized them more or less to the exclusion of less congenial teachings. Some of Jesus' teachings, such as we find in these parables, do have definite implications of gradual growth. It is hard to see how they can be interpreted otherwise. However, they do not necessarily imply *social* growth or progress; they may refer only to the individual's growth in faith. The parable of the sower seems most naturally interpreted as a description of what happens to various individuals when they are confronted by the faith. The attempt to interpret these passages as predictions of evolutionary progress may be more the result of wish thinking than of fact.

There is, however, one major parable that does denote gradual growth, but not progress in the sense of the progressive victory of good over evil; and it certainly includes apocalyptic judgment. It is the parable of the wheat and the weeds (tares). It is found in its full form only in Matthew (ch. 13: 24-30). In this parable there is obviously growth of the wheat, but there is also growth of the weeds. The two grow equally together, and the " householder " refuses to let his servants pull out the weeds, " ' lest in gathering the weeds you root up the wheat along with them. Let both grow together until the harvest; and at harvest time I will tell the reapers, Gather the weeds first and bind them in bundles to be burned, but gather the wheat into my barn.'" Thus, there are in the teachings of Jesus a definite implication of growth, but it is not of gradually easing into a perfect society. It is growth until the "harvest"—a definite and sudden end.

(*c*) *The Kingdom of God is here now.* Against the idea that the Kingdom is something coming in the future there is also the idea that in some sense the Kingdom is here now. It is a state into which one can enter now, if one chooses and is ready to fulfill the requirements, without having to wait until the end of history. Although this understanding of the nature of the Kingdom is much more explicitly expressed in John's Gospel (chs. 3: 1-8; 5: 20-24; 9; 17) it is also implicit in the Synoptics. There is the constant note that the Kingdom "is at hand"; Jesus tells the "sympathetic scribe," "You are not far from the kingdom of God" (Mark 12: 34). It is a treasure hidden in a field or a pearl of great price which a person can get *now* by selling all that he has to buy it (Matt. 13: 44-46). When asked when the Kingdom would come, Jesus replied, "The kingdom of God is not coming with signs to be observed; nor will they say, 'Lo, here it is!' or 'There!' for behold, the kingdom of God is in the midst of you" (Luke 17: 20-21). At the conclusion of his reply to the charge that he cast out demons by Beelzebub, Jesus said: "But if it is by the finger of God that I cast out demons, then the kingdom of God has come upon you" (Luke 11: 20). In view of these and other passages it is undeniable that Jesus taught that the Kingdom is, in some sense, here now.

Thus, it is quite clear from the records that Jesus taught both that the Kingdom is coming in the future and that it is a present reality. This dual emphasis has created some difficulty. Technically this is known as the question: "futuristic eschatology" versus "realized eschatology." The word "eschatology" means the study or knowledge of "last things," or of "the end." "Futuristic eschatology" emphasizes, points to, and attempts to describe the end of history when the Kingdom of God will be finally and completely established. "Realized eschatology" describes the way the Kingdom is present now and how one can enter into it now. Both of these emphases are found not only in the teachings of Jesus but also in all of the New Testament. Both, as we shall see below, are essential to Christian faith and a Christian philosophy of history, but first their relevance needs to be made clear for moderns.

4. The Significance of the Kingdom as Coming

The Biblical emphasis on futuristic eschatology — on the end of history, which is frequently described in exceedingly catastrophic terms — has proved very disturbing to most moderns. With the advent of Biblical criticism which undermined the literal interpretation of the Bible and with the advent of modern science and the evolutionary theory which conclusively demonstrated that the world is millions of years older, and presumably will continue for millions of more years, than was previously thought, it became almost impossible for modern educated people to think of the end, especially in Biblical terms. The result has been, at least among the "enlightened," either to ignore or to deny the Biblical doctrine. Today, however, we may be a little more ready to admit that this bypassing of a fundamental Biblical position may have been a little too hasty.

First, and really a minor point: Although nature, left more or less to itself, probably would continue to leave the earth an inhabitable place for millions of years to come, the discovery of atomic fission by man may upset nature's timetable. We know now that we live under the threat of extinction at a moment's notice from atomic destruction. The writer would not belabor the point lest he be accused of Bibliolatry, but it is interesting to note how closely some of the Biblical descriptions of the end fit the description of atomic explosions. Wrote the writer of II Peter: "Then the heavens will pass away with a loud noise, and the elements will be dissolved with fire, and the earth and the works that are upon it will be burned up" (ch. 3:10). To draw attention to such Biblical statements is not to imply that the Biblical writers were predicting atomic destruction in our time and it is not to imply that the Bible says that man will blow himself up in the twentieth century A.D. Biblically speaking, nothing can be a more stupid waste of time than trying to figure out when the end will come. The Bible is emphatic that no one knows. Even Jesus is reported to have said: "But of that day and hour no one knows, not even the angels of heaven, nor the Son, but the Father only" (Matt. 24:36; Mark 13:32; see also Acts 1:6-7). All that the Bible says, and it says it unequivocally, is that there will be an end with judgment.

That there will be an end is the really important event which moderns had largely forgotten until the discovery of atomic fission forceably reminded us of that possibility in our own time. Under the impetus of evolution and a too superficial doctrine of progress most people looked to an indefinite and increasingly rosy future. If there were to be an end someday, some millions of years hence when the sun cooled off, it was too far away to consider. To the secular the Biblical insistence on an end was merely another proof of the unreliability of the Bible; to the more pious it was an embarrassment which they tried to get around with the aid of Biblical criticism. But the Biblical doctrine of the end is still there and in this as in many other areas the Bible is profoundly right.

There must be an end. An endless progression is a meaningless concept and a doctrine of the end is necessary for any adequate philosophy of history. Atomic bombs aside, scientifically speaking there will be an end sometime, if only when the sun cools off, although it may be delayed a long, long time. However, in principle —and this is the really important fact—*in principle it does not matter whether the end comes in our time via atomic destruction, or some millions of years hence by some other method. There will be an end*. This is the fact to which the Bible points. If the end should come in our time, it may be more exciting for us, but that does not change the principle. There has to be a "last generation" sometime, and any adequate philosophy of history has to have a doctrine of the end. One of the reasons why people are so terrified by the thought of atomic destruction today is that they have refused to have a philosophy of the end, to say nothing of understanding the Biblical doctrine.

It is to the necessity of the end that the Biblical doctrine of the Kingdom as coming points. But the Biblical idea of the Kingdom of God not only points to the fact that there will be an end; it also insists that the end, the final conclusion, will be good. It will be the Kingdom of God, the Kingdom or Reign of a God who knows what is really good and can bring it about. The Biblical description of the Kingdom of God, or the New Jerusalem with pearly gates, should not be taken literally. These descriptions are simply human attempts to affirm, within the limitations of language and the ancient culture, the essential principle of the Christian faith, namely, that the end will be good because God is the kind of God revealed in Jesus Christ.

The Biblical descriptions of the end also include judgment. Before and in connection with the end there will be a Final Judgment. In Chapter III, on the nature of God, we have considered the necessity of his being a Judge. This idea now needs to be related to the Final Judgment at the end of history.

Among the early casualties of the combination of empirical science and Biblical criticism were the descriptions of a Final Judgment and of heaven and hell in any literal sense. The concepts of heaven and hell have been fairly successfully reinterpreted for the modern mind. The idea of a Last and Final Judgment has proved to be more difficult. Most " emancipated " persons reject it or simply ignore it. It is surprising how little reference to it is made by twentieth-century Christian writers, except among the Fundamentalists. What was once a vivid and central element of Christian faith has become almost extinct, although the Evanston Ecumenical Conference has happily revived some interest in this question.

The simple fact is that without the idea of a Final Judgment it is impossible to establish any real meaning for history or for life, and it is certainly impossible to establish any validity for anything other than a completely relativistic ethics. In our discussion of the resurrection much was said that would be relevant here. For purposes of presentation in this book it seemed better to discuss the resurrection in connection with the work of Christ. However, it should not be forgotten that in the New Testament when it speaks of the coming Kingdom, resurrection and judgment are usually combined. This is a profound and true revelation. Just, as we have seen, as there can be no solution to the tragedy of human existence without a resurrection, neither can there be a solution to the tragic frustrations of history without a Final Judgment. Unless somewhere, sometime, somehow, there is a judgment that goes beyond human judgment, separates the good from the evil, overcomes and destroys the evil and establishes the good, there is not much sense in anything at all. Certainly there is no sense in trying to do the good when it requires self-sacrifice. Thus, the idea of a Final Judgment that is more than a human judgment (for all men are finite, fallible, and sinners) is absolutely essential to give life and history meaning, and to validate any ethics.

The New Testament consistently maintains such a point of view and where this idea is lost both life and ethics deteriorate. As we pointed out above, it is very significant that in the twentieth century, when both the ideas of resurrection and of Final Judgment have gone into an eclipse, we find the rise of a debilitating relativism and of ruthless dehumanizing nationalism and totalitarianism. If there be no Final Judgment before which men must stand, why not exploit everyone as shrewdly as possible? Or, for the more timid whose ultimate philosophy is, "I'll scratch your back if you scratch mine," why not do what everyone else does just to be as comfortable as possible? "When in Rome do as the Romans do!" becomes the ultimate criterion of ethics—if there is no Final Judgment.

It is ridiculous to speculate on what the Final Judgment will be like. All attempts to describe it are simply human attempts to describe the indescribable. Even the writer of the Revelation of John, who went farthest in description, declares: "And when the seven thunders had sounded, I was about to write, but I heard a voice from heaven saying, 'Seal up what the seven thunders have said, and do not write it down'" (Rev. 10:4). It is a "mystery of God" (Rev. 10:7). This much can be said and this is what all the symbolism points to: There will be a Final Judgment in which evil is destroyed permanently and good is established permanently. This is possible because the Judge will be no finite being but God or Christ.[66]

A. *Predestination, Heaven and Hell*

What happens after the Final Judgment can be a very baffling question. It is involved with the whole problem of predestination or election and what is called "the double decree." The New Testament, with its obvious use over and over again of terms like "chosen," "elected," "called," "foreordained," and so forth, clearly maintains a doctrine of predestination. According to this doctrine God elects some for salvation and the rest, by hypothesis, are elected for damnation; at least God is responsible for their damnation in that he did not elect them for salvation. This is why it is sometimes called "the double decree." But this doctrine admittedly has repulsive features which seem to destroy the goodness of God. The only logical alternative is that God elects everyone for salvation. Thus, throughout the history of the Church, there has been a debate couched in the terms of "double decree" versus "universalism."

We cannot here go into all the intricacies of the doctrine of predestination. This much, however, needs to be said: It is in the Bible and there is no use pretending it is not. As a thoroughly Biblical doctrine it must be faced and reckoned with. How we work out the details may be debatable, but fundamentally the doctrine points to a profound Christian truth which cannot be given up without giving up what is essential to our faith. And that truth is that God is in control of his world; not only did he create it, but he is in control of it, and he will bring it to a good conclusion — the Kingdom of God. In order to be in control of the end, it is necessary to be in control of the intermediate steps along the way and the means to the end, for the intermediate steps and the means ultimately determine the nature of the end.

Not only does the Bible speak of predestination; it also says emphatically in many places that only those who believe in Christ are saved — the rest are damned. Even if we take the description of the fiery fate of the damned as only symbols and say we do not really know what ultimate damnation is, except perhaps perpetual alienation from God, it is still a very terrible fate. This seems inconsistent with the Biblical revelation of God as revealed in Jesus Christ, because no one asked to be born, and if God created everything, he then created all souls and he is therefore responsible for this damnation. The thesis often put forward, that God after creating us gives us freedom of choice and we are responsible for our own "bad choices," does not altogether solve the question; for not only did we not ask to be born, but also we did not ask to be born into a world where these momentous choices with such terrible consequences have to be made. It looks as though the only real choice is the choice Hitler gave the Germans — to vote "*Ja!*" or be liquidated! The Roman Church tries partially to solve this question by the invention of the un-Biblical doctrine of purgatory, into which most souls go (since very, very few persons are all good or all bad) for an indefinite period of purification. But the concept of purgatory does not solve the problem; it only delays it. Even though the Roman Church assumes that almost everyone is ultimately purifiable after a sufficient stay in purgatory and that only a very few go to hell, as long as one single solitary soul is damned the problem remains.

Throughout the history of the Church sensitive souls have struggled with this question. Origen, an Early Church Father, held out hope that, if not in this world, then in some later world, all would be saved. Saint Augustine held the opposite point of view. He developed the most rigorous post-Biblical doctrine of predestination and unequivocally declared that God elected for salvation only those whom he chose and the rest were damned as, said Saint Augustine, they deserved to be. By and large, the Church has held to a more or less Augustinian position although usually much less rigorously, and there have been exceptions like Duns Scotus. Among Protestants, Calvin, as all know, followed Saint

Augustine most closely, and predestination has been a factor in Calvinistic thought. Luther, according to Emil Brunner, after initially taking a rather extreme predestinarian view later somewhat mitigated it.[67] Modern Protestant thought, at least in liberal circles, has found the doctrine repugnant and for the most part has ignored or bypassed it. It is interesting to note, however, that as conservative a theologian as Karl Barth tends toward the universalist position, and believes that since Christ has taken on himself the condemnation of all sin for all people, therefore even the godless who reject Christ will not be ultimately rejected.[68] Brunner disagrees with Barth.

Brunner criticizes Barth severely, partly on the grounds that Barth's universalism is "in absolute opposition — and this alone is the final objection to it — to the clear teaching of the New Testament" (p. 349). But Brunner is also more than a little appalled at the idea of eternal damnation for anyone. He wants to be true to what he believes is the Biblical revelation, and at the same time he wants to reject the "double decree" theory. He tries to resolve the dilemma by what he calls the paradox of faith, but his position, to this writer, is more ambiguous or inconsistent than it is a paradox. On page 338 he writes of the "paradox of faith that God in Christ has elected all who believe in him, but not those who refuse to give him the obedience of faith. . . . This . . . decision, which is Faith or Unbelief, is a matter of life or death, heaven or hell, of real deliverance or the real possibility of being lost." But on page 353 he writes: "No doctrine taught in the Bible, least of all that of salvation in Christ, is given to us in order that we should think out what is purposed for those who do not accept salvation." To my mind these statements, if not actually contradictory, are certainly very ambiguous. What Brunner most wants to do is to preserve the freedom of human decisions and their consequences. He sees that *logically* once one starts with the Christian presuppositions about the nature of God as Creator and Arbiter of destiny one is driven either to universalism or to the "double decree." In either case, logically, human freedom to decide is destroyed, for in either case it has all been foreordained in advance. So he also criticizes Barth on the grounds that Barth's universalism is just as destructive of the significance of decision as the "double decree" theory. He writes: "We must absolutely resist the inclination to draw 'logical conclusions,' since they only lead to one of two errors: either the doctrine of the 'double decree,' or to the doctrine of universal salvation, each of which removes the reality of the decision of faith" (p. 353).

Brunner here recognizes what is an old, old question, and that is: What is the relation of human freedom to God's control? By what he calls the "paradox" of faith and by deliberately denying the need for being logical, he preserves the possibility of a free human decision. The importance of this decision, he declares, is known only in faith. "Outside of faith man knows nothing of this, but he lives, taking things very much for granted. . . . Faith alone knows the abyss from which Christ saves" (p. 339). If this is true, what happens to the man who is "outside of faith," the unbeliever, and especially the man who has never heard of Christ or that there is a decision of faith to be made? This is a real question and it needs a real answer which Brunner evades.

In the writer's own attempt to answer it, he would point out that when Brunner declares, "The Bible does not speak of universal salvation, but on the contrary of judgment and of twofold destiny: salvation and doom" (p. 352), he is making too sweeping a statement. As we have noted, there certainly are many passages which appear to justify such a statement, but there are also passages which point definitely to a different conclusion. To cite a few of these universalist passages: "For God has consigned all men to disobedience, that he may have mercy upon all"—*not some, but all!* (Rom. 11:32.) And it is not without significance that this is Paul's conclusion to the most complete discussion of predestination and election in the New Testament. To this can be added: "For there is one God, and there is one mediator between God and men, the man Christ Jesus, who gave himself as a ransom for all." (I Tim. 2:5-6.) "That at the name of Jesus every knee should bow, in heaven and on earth and under the earth, and every tongue confess that Jesus Christ is Lord." (Phil.

2:10-11.) Perhaps less explicit but still implicitly significant is: "All things were created through him and for him. He is before all things, and in him all things hold together." (Col. 1:16-18.) Among the teachings of Jesus there is the story of the rich young ruler who rejects Jesus. Our Lord, after commenting on how hard it is for a rich man to enter the Kingdom of God, goes on to add, "What is impossible with men is possible with God" (Luke 18:27). And then there is his famous reply to the question of the Sadducees about the resurrection: "He is not God of the dead, but of the living; for all live to him." (Luke 20:38.) Brunner's emphatic statement that the Bible does not speak of universal salvation is too sweeping.

The simple fact is that in the New Testament there are two sets of teachings about the ultimate destiny of man. The larger number are certainly of the "double decree" variety, but the more universal-salvation teachings are there too. And there may be a good sociological-psychological explanation for the preponderance of emphasis on doom for unbelievers. We must remember that the Church at the time most of the New Testament was being written was undergoing various degrees of persecution from social ostracism and denial of civil rights to downright martyrdom. To become a Christian in those days was a very risky business. It is an almost inevitable human reaction that when we are penalized (particularly when we feel it unjust), a desire for vengeance arises. This may be regrettable but it is human, and the more severe the penalization the more severe we want "the squaring of accounts." But Christians are not supposed to take vengeance; rather, they are to love their enemies and pray for those who persecute them (Matt. 5:44). That the early Christians were able to succeed as well as they did in the actual practice of loving their enemies is a tremendous tribute to their faith, patience, and will power. But becoming a Christian does not completely overcome human nature. It is inevitable that Christians, some unconsciously but probably many consciously, felt a deep desire for vengeance. If, because of the requirements of their faith, or from sheer inability to retaliate against their persecutors, they could not see "justice done" in this world, it is not surprising that they wanted to see it done in the next world—and done thoroughly! Even the great Paul seems to have accepted this, and he must have felt that one way to ensure the practice of the Christian virtues among his followers in this world was to assure them that the accounts would be balanced in the next. "Repay no one evil for evil, but take thought for what is noble in the sight of all. . . . Beloved, never avenge yourselves, but leave it to the wrath of God; for it is written, 'Vengeance is mine, I will repay, says the Lord.' No, 'if your enemy is hungry, feed him; if he is thirsty, give him drink; for by so doing you will heap burning coals upon his head.'" (Rom. 12:17, 19-20.) Certainly some and probably a lot of the condemnation of unbelievers in the New Testament arises from the human desire of people who have unjustly suffered, sometimes terribly, wanting to see the accounts balanced.

Some—but not all of it! Justice—and God is constantly portrayed in the Bible as a God of justice—requires that there be a righting of wrongs and the defeat of evil, and this is what the Biblical accounts of the Last Judgment, the salvation of the saints, and the damnation of the wicked affirm. In this sense the "double decree," if not a literal description, is symbolically valid. But how is it to be reconciled with the universal-salvation line of thought which is also valid? The best solution of this problem is that of the late Nicolas Berdyaev in his *The Destiny of Man*.[69]

In that discussion Berdyaev maintains we must understand the Christian conceptions of heaven and hell from two different perspectives at the same time. We must consider them from both the human and the divine points of view, both of which are necessary for a full understanding and both of which are also necessarily different, for man is not God. From the human point of view the ideas of heaven and of hell are absolutely essential. It is absolutely essential for human thought, decision, and action, especially for the validation of any ethics other than sheer relativity, that there be a real distinction between good and evil and that the good ultimately triumph over the evil. Heaven stands for the victory of the good, and hell stands for the destruction of the evil. From the human point of view this is a *sine qua non* in order to make any sense out of life at all. But from God's point of view the idea of heaven, and especially the idea of hell as a place or state of eternal damnation, is utterly impossible. As we have noted before, no one asks to be born; no one volunteers to take on this life with its agonizing decisions full of such eternal consequences. If God has created, or permitted to be created, one single soul which he would not or could not save, then that is a denial of the meaning of the cross, the incarnation, the atonement, and the whole revelation of Jesus Christ. Thus, a place is made for both judgment and universal salvation, both of which are necessary, as the Bible correctly affirms. It seems to the writer that this is what Paul meant when he wrote: "For no other foundation can anyone lay than that which is laid, which is Jesus Christ. Now if anyone builds on the foundation with gold, silver, precious stones, wood, hay, stubble—each man's work . . . will be revealed with fire, and the fire will test what sort of work each one has done. If the work which any man has built on the foundation survives, he will receive a reward. If any man's work is burned up, he will suffer loss, though he himself will be saved, but only as through fire." (I Cor. 3: 11-15.)

If it is claimed that this interpretation removes the necessity and importance of the human decision, and that there is no need to do or decide anything because everyone is to be saved in the long run anyway, the writer can only reply that such a claim, although widespread, is based upon a profound misunderstanding of the Christian, and as has been shown, the Biblical faith. Throughout this book the importance of the eternal has been emphasized: we are citizens of two worlds at once and of the two our citizenship in the eternal world is ultimately far more important. In this sense our life in this world can best be described as being "on a pilgrimage." Nevertheless, while we live we are in this world, and as long as we live we have to live in it. *Christ came into this world*. He came not to sell a kind of celestial fire insurance but that men might have life and have it abundantly — here and now as well as hereafter. The purpose of being a Christian is not to escape hell's fires but to live a creative and abundant life now. We who are Christians believe that we achieve our true and most creative (and therefore most joyous) destiny only as we submit our lives to the God revealed in Jesus Christ, in whom alone is perfect freedom. To fail to do this is to miss the mark, no matter how successful we may appear to be outwardly. And this involves a decision and a choice of the utmost consequences. It is, indeed, a decision of life or death, *but it is a decision in this world,* which is really all we know about. Concerning the next world — we know that it is there, and we confidently trust the God revealed in Jesus Christ to bring it to a good conclusion in terms that God knows are good.

5. The Significance of the Kingdom as Here Now

If the validity of the Biblical idea of the Kingdom as coming in the future at the end of history has been established, it is now time to examine briefly the other side of Jesus' thought about the Kingdom, namely, that it is in some sense present, and that we can enter it in this life without having to wait for the end of history. We have already seen that this is clearly one of Jesus' emphases about the Kingdom. But what does it mean and in what sense is the Kingdom here?

Obviously neither in Jesus' time nor at any time since has there been any noticeable reduction in suffering, injustice, and tragedy. People still suffer and die. There is still tragedy and frustration; there is still heartache. And if one thinks in terms of man's inhumanity to man, the twentieth century is as black as any previous one. If what was said about man as sinner in Chapter IV is true, this situation will continue to the end of history. How then can anyone say that the Kingdom is here now?

In view of this tragic situation it is obvious that the Kingdom is not here now in the sense that we have a perfect utopian society. The ultimate establishment of that state is what "futuristic eschatology" refers to; "realized eschatology," the idea that it is possible to enter the Kingdom in the present, refers to something quite different. In general, the Christian Church has believed that the Kingdom is here now in two senses: one personal and one social, although never social in the sense of all of society being in it.

Perhaps as good a passage as any to illustrate what is meant by entering the Kingdom on the personal level is the story reported in the Synoptics where Jesus' mother and brothers came to him, apparently to dissuade him. He is told they are outside waiting for him and he replies: "Who are my mother and my brothers? . . . Whoever does the will of God is my brother, and sister, and mother" (Mark 3: 33, 35). It is the testimony of generations of Christians that when we submit ourselves to God in Christ, try to be obedient to him, and honestly seek to do his will as we see it, we do enter into a whole new state: "If any one is in Christ, he is a new creation [or creature]" (II Cor. 5: 17). The world does not change. Its tragedies still remain, but we meet them with a new power — a power not of ourselves. This is an actual possibility now and to accept and fulfill that possibility is to enter into the Kingdom.

There is another but related sense in which, at the personal level, we can also enter the Kingdom. Life, as we experience it, comes to us in an endless series of times, or moments, or situations, and then they are gone.[70] But each of these situations contains certain potentialities or possibilities; and the possibilities of one situation differ from those of another. Some may be quite insignificant, as, for instance, how we greet a person on the street; while others may be very important, as, how we make a decision that will affect our lifework, or the lives of other people. In any case, our lives are made up of successive moments or situations with possibilities that must be met well or badly. According to our Christian faith, God is the Lord of all life; in each of these situations there is always a God-given possibility which is the best possibility. In so far as we fulfill the possibilities of a given situation according to the will of God as we understand it, we live in the Kingdom of God for that moment. This is a real possibility and at the moment we can live in the Kingdom, for to live in the Kingdom is to live according to the will of God. Then that situation passes and in the next we may and probably do fail to a greater or lesser extent. Certainly none of us meets all situations according to the will of God, and most of us only rarely; therefore we live in the Kingdom only rarely or fragmentarily. Nevertheless, it can be a real living in the Kingdom in this world.

There is also a sense in which the Kingdom is here as a social group. Ernst Troeltsch in his discussion of the gospel ethic rightly declares that, "Its [the gospel's teaching on the Kingdom] first outstanding characteristic is an unlimited, unqualified, individualism," but "this absolute religious individualism . . . also contains within it a strong idea of fellowship, . . . a fellowship of love among those who are united in God, . . . the union of those who are united in God."[71] The Church has always affirmed that within its fellowship there exists a present and real earnest of the Kingdom of God. The very idea that the Church is the Body of Christ presupposes that as the Kingdom was made manifest in the body of Christ in his earthly life, it continues to be manifest in the fellowship of those united in him, which is the Church. "For where two or three are gathered in my name, there am I in the midst of them." (Matt. 18:20.) And where Christ is, there the Kingdom is. That this is true and that in the Church we do actually enter the Kingdom is the testimony of multitudes of Christians of all ages.

If one thinks seriously about this dual aspect of the Kingdom of God, as both coming and as present, it will be discovered that this is precisely what all men need in order to live at their most creative and most courageous best. All men need at least two things in order to work creatively and satisfactorily at any task. They need the hope that their efforts will be ultimately vindicated sometime, even if not in their own lifetime; and they need the sense of some realization of that hope in the present. Certainly no one but a masochist makes sacrifices for something that he feels is utterly futile and purposeless. Human nature needs hope in the ultimate vindication of its goals in order to work creatively, and with self-sacrifice which is necessary for life in this world. At the same time only the rarest saint will work constructively at something for which he sees no possibility of even approximate realization in his own lifetime. Most of us need some prospect of achievement now in order to keep going. The dual concept of the Kingdom as both future and present fulfills both these needs. Because the Kingdom of God is the Kingdom *of God* we know that it will ultimately come, but in the meantime we do not have to wait for it until the end which may be eons away. Here and now as we work for it we enter into it and receive some of its rewards. Thus, again, we see how the Biblical Christian faith meets the existential needs of man.

6. The Christian Philosophy of History

We are perhaps now in a position to examine more critically the Christian philosophy of history. Any philosophy of history other than the one that there can be no philosophy of history must fulfill certain requirements in order to be intellectually respectable. It must give meaning to all of historical existence and must give a perspective for judging the various phases and facets of historical existence. In order to do this it must, as we have seen, guarantee a " good conclusion " which becomes the criterion for the judging of various phases of history. But the " good conclusion " must be grounded in more than a pious hope and wish thinking; it must be grounded in an existential historical fact. This existential historical fact thus becomes the " center of meaning " (although it need not be, and indeed can only momentarily be, the chronological center) which both points to the " good conclusion " and illumines the phases of history. Finally, this center of meaning must be preserved in a " historical group " or " institution " which preserves, represents, and carries it on through history. If this does not happen, the philosophy will be lost and thereby be proved not to be a valid interpretation of history.

There may be other philosophies of history that fulfill all these requirements but I do not know of them. The Christian philosophy of history does fulfill them. The "good conclusion" which gives life meaning and becomes the criterion of judgment is the Kingdom of God which is coming with judgment. (It is significant that no matter how good a social situation is, when we compare it with the Kingdom of God we are forced to say, "This is not it.") That the "good conclusion" is not merely an illusion and pious wish thinking is demonstrated in the historical fact of Jesus Christ, the incarnation of God, who entered history and proclaimed (revealed) the Kingdom as God's intention for the world. Thus, Jesus Christ and his work become the "center of meaning." All phases of history can be judged and interpreted in terms of this center. For instance, in the light of Jesus Christ as the center of meaning for history the primitive and non-Christian religions are understood as preparation for the reception of Jesus Christ. Reinhold Niebuhr has somewhere observed: "Nothing is more absurd than the answer to an unasked question." Christ answers the basic questions of the meaning of human existence — human existence finds meaning in salvation, in the Kingdom of God which Christ has already revealed. Before, however, Christ, the answer, will even be listened to, people must be ready to ask the right question. All religions — and all the philosophies too, for that matter — are built upon raising and trying to answer the questions of the meaning of existence. Therefore they prepare people for asking the questions to which Christ is the answer. Even secularism, where Christ is temporarily rejected, can be understood and interpreted, not as meaningless patterns that do not fit in, but rather as temporary rejections that will be overcome eventually (Phil. 2:9-11). Finally, in the history of this world, the revelation of Christ is received, preserved, and perpetuated from generation to generation by the fellowship of those who are united in Christ, that is, the Church, the Body of Christ, marching down through the ages and spreading throughout the world until the Kingdom comes.

Notes

[1] *Concluding Unscientific Postscript,* in *A Kierkegaard Anthology,* edited by Robert Bretall, p. 213. Princeton University Press, 1946. Also, Paul Tillich writes: "Not only he who is in sin but he who is in doubt is justified through faith. The situation of doubt, even doubt about God, need not separate us from God." *The Protestant Era,* p. xiv. University of Chicago Press, 1948.

[2] Henry N. Wieman, *Directive in History,* pp. 20, 25, 26; see also p. 132. Free Press, 1949.

[3] Alan Richardson, *Christian Apologetics,* pp. 235-236. Harper & Brothers, 1947.

[4] Arthur Koestler, *Arrival and Departure,* pp. 177–178. The Macmillan Company, 1943. Used by permission.

[5] Julian Huxley, *The Biologist Looks at Man,* quoted in *Modern Exposition,* edited by William Davenport and Paul Bowerman, p. 146. Harcourt, Brace and Company, Inc., 1946.

[6] *Religio Medici,* quoted in *The Interpreter's Bible* Vol. I, pp. 874-875. Abingdon Press, 1952.

[7] J. S. Whale, *The Christian Doctrine,* p. 26. The Macmillan Company, 1941.

[8] Paul Tillich, *Systematic Theology,* Vol. I, pp. 204-205. University of Chicago Press, 1951.

[9] Emil Brunner, *Our Faith,* translated by John W. Rilling, p. 13. Charles Scribner's Sons, 1949.

[10] Tillich, *op. cit.,* especially Part II.

[11] Eric Frank, *Philosophical Understanding and Religious Truth,* translated by Professor and Mrs. Ludwitz Edelstein, p. 44. Oxford University Press, 1945.

[12] Herbert Spiegelberg, "Supernaturalism and Naturalism: A Study in Meaning and Verifiability," in *Philosophy of Science,* Vol. 18, No. 4, p. 345.

13 Rudolf Otto, *The Idea of the Holy,* translated by John W. Harvey. Oxford University Press, 1950.

14 Whale, *op. cit.,* p. 27.

15 *The Interpreter's Bible,* Vol. X, p. 425. Abingdon Press, 1953.

16 Arthur S. Peake, ed., *Commentary on the Bible,* p. 723. Thomas Nelson & Sons. *Peake's Commentary,* p. 723. C. T. and E. C. Jack, Ltd.

17 A. J. Toynbee, *Study of History,* Vol. VI, pp. 47-48. Oxford University Press, 1939.

18 The weakness of Zoroastrianism is that Ahura-Mazda is not really the lord of history. He must share his power with and fight against Angra Mainya, thus, the solution in Zoroastrianism is destruction and not fulfillment. See Paul Tillich's *The Protestant Era,* p. 20. University of Chicago Press.

19 Tillich, *Systematic Theology,* Vol. I, p. 215.

20 Reinhold Niebuhr, *The Nature and Destiny of Man, II,* pp. 23-26. Charles Scribner's Sons, 1943.

21 Gustaf Aulén, *The Faith of the Christian Church,* translated by Erich H. Wahlstrom and G. Everett Arden, p. 198. Muhlenberg Press, 1948.

22 *Ibid.,* p. 199.

23 This statement is not intended to deny the significance of a "life beyond this life." A "life beyond this life" is implicit in the supranatural position, and its significance will be considered in Chapter VI.

24 For this illustration I am indebted to William A. Spurrier's *Power for Action.* Charles Scribner's Sons, 1948.

25 The temporariness of all forms of human creativity needs emphasis. Man tends to exaggerate the permanence of his constructions. He does this because at a deeper and often unconscious level he is aware that his constructions are not so permanent as he wishes. And as far as the individual is concerned all his constructions end for him at his death.

26 Sören Kierkegaard, *The Concept of Dread,* translated by Walter Lowry, pp. 37 f. and 54 f. Princeton University Press, 1944.

27 Paul Tillich, *The Shaking of the Foundations,* pp. 42, 45. Charles Scribner's Sons, 1949.

28 This attitude is still strong. In most colleges where religion is

taught at all there is a course in "The Life and Teachings of Jesus."

29 The generally accepted approximate dates are: Mark, A.D. 70; Luke, A.D. 80; Matthew, A.D. 85; John, A.D. 95 or later.

30 Robert C. Johnson, "The Jesus of History and the Christ of Faith," in *Theology Today*, July, 1953, p. 171.

31 *Ibid.*, p. 182.

32 Since the fact of the resurrection is the most important and most debatable of all these facts it will be treated in a special section later.

33 H. Butterfield, *Christianity and History*, p. 3. Charles Scribner's Sons, 1950.

34 For my own attempt to wrestle with this problem, see my *Thinking Christianly*, Ch. VI. The Macmillan Company, 1948.

35 H. G. Wells, *Outline of History*, one vol. ed., p. 509. Garden City Books, 1921.

36 Harry Emerson Fosdick, "Faith and Immortality," in the *Union Seminary Quarterly Review*, May, 1953.

37 The fact that the end of Mark's Gospel stops or has been lost before relating an actual resurrection appearance does not negate this position. See Mark 16: 1–8; also ch. 1:1 which establishes Mark's thesis.

38 Rudolf Bultmann in his *Theology of the New Testament* (Charles Scribner's Sons, 1951) has a minute but illuminating discussion of Paul's use of the word "body." He points out that Paul uses two different Greek words, *sarx* and *soma*. Although occasionally the two words are interchangeable, generally *sarx* means flesh, or physical body in the usual sense. *Soma*, also translated "body," is "most complex and the understanding of it is fraught with difficulty" (Vol. I, p. 192). But it is not to be confused with *sarx*. "Man is called *soma* in respect to his being able to make himself the object of his own action or to experience himself as the subject to whom something happens. He can be called *soma*, that is, having a relationship to himself" (pp. 195-196). "Man, his person as a whole, can be denoted by *soma*. It may also be significant that Paul never calls a corpse *soma*, though such usage is found both in profane Greek and in the LXX (Septuagint translation of the Old Testament)" (p. 195).

39 Using the marginal reading of the RSV and the regular reading

of the KJV and ASV, Peake's *Commentary* makes this even more emphatic, using the word "within," p. 558.

[40] Robert Bretall, ed., *A Kierkegaard Anthology*, p. 209.

[41] Our analysis is oversimple for lack of space. Actually immortality of the soul in one form or another is widespread among ancient religions, but significantly the ancient Hebrews held a very dim view of life after death. (See many of the psalms.)

[42] Paul Tillich, *The Shaking of the Foundations*, p. 172.

[43] Karl Barth, *Dogmatics in Outline*, pp. 117-118. Philosophical Library, Inc., 1947.

[44] Omar Khayyām, *The Rubáiyát*, verse LXXXI, FitzGerald translation. See also Job 1: 20-24; 10: 1-22.

[45] Gustaf Aulén, *Christus Victor*, p. 21. The Macmillan Company, 1931.

[46] *Ibid.*, p. 20.

[47] *Ibid.*, p. 171.

[48] H. P. Van Dusen, ed., *The Christian Answer*, pp. 117–118. Charles Scribner's Sons, 1945.

[49] *The Westminster Study Edition of The Holy Bible* (The Westminster Press, 1948) commenting on Matt. 16: 13-20 says that the word translated here as "church" is used in the Greek O. T. of the congregation of Israel; Jesus may have used it rarely of the true Israel of God he was building" (New Testament, p. 50).

[50] No matter how distasteful the doctrine of election is to moderns it is evident on almost every page of the New Testament. See Ch. VIII, sec. 4, A.

[51] Gustaf Aulén, *The Faith of the Christian Church*, p. 336.

[52] Aulén (in *The Faith of the Christian Church*, p. 381) argues persuasively, but not in my opinion convincingly, that infant Baptism is the highest expression of Baptism.

[53] J. B. Phillips, *Appointment with God*, p. 12. The Macmillan Company, 1954.

[54] John Dillenberger and Claude Welch, *Protestant Christianity Interpreted Through Its Development*, p. 52. Charles Scribner's Sons, 1954.

[55] *Ibid.*, p. 51.

[56] C. S. Lewis, *The Screwtape Letters*, p. 15. The Macmillan Company, 1943.

[57] Toynbee, *op. cit.*, Vol. V, p. 23.

[58] There had already been the great split in the Church between East and West in 1054.

[59] Paul Tillich, *The Shaking of the Foundations,* Chapter 1.

[60] Morris Cohen, *The Meaning of Human History,* p. 267. The Open Court Publishing Company, 1947.

[61] Toynbee, *op. cit.,* Vol. IV, p. 7.

[62] *Ibid.,* p. 34.

[63] Plato's *Republic* was written primarily not to portray a "perfect society" but to illustrate human nature and defend the ideal of virtue. In any event, Plato went on to show that the republic would inevitably break down.

[64] Quoted by Reinhold Niebuhr in *The Nature and Destiny of Man, II,* p. 26, n. 13.

[65] The word "apocalyptic" means "unveiling" or "revelation" of future events, usually having to do with the end of the world, or age. The Revelation to John is the chief example of apocalyptic writing in the New Testament.

[66] The term "judge" in the New Testament is applied somewhat indiscriminatingly to both God and Christ. This, of course, is because the New Testament always assumes that Christ is God incarnate.

[67] Emil Brunner, *The Christian Doctrine of God,* translated by Olive Wyon, pp. 342-345. The Westminster Press, 1950.

[68] *Ibid.* See especially the appendix "Karl Barth's Doctrine of Election," pp. 346-353.

[69] Nicolas Berdyaev, *The Destiny of Man.* Geoffrey Bles, Ltd., London, 1945.

[70] I am obviously here indebted to Paul Tillich's idea of the *Kairos.*

[71] Ernst Troeltsch, *The Social Teaching of the Christian Churches,* translated by Olive Wyon, Vol. I, pp. 55-56. The Macmillan Company, 1931.

Index

Abélard, 132
aloneness, 81, 86 ff.
Angst, 80 ff., 86–87
Anselm, 51, 52, 132
apologetic, 15
apostolic succession, 144–145
arts, the, 38–39
assumptions, 22–24, 27, 29
atheism, atheists, 18, 47, 93, 94
atonement, 27, 129 ff., 135
  theories of, 131–134
Auden, W. H., 161
Augustine, 89, 177
Aulén, Gustaf, 73, 74, 133–134, 144, 149 f. n.

baptism, 142, 148–149
Barth, Karl, 102, 118, 178 ff.
Becker, C. L., 164
Berdyaev, Nicolas, 181
Berkeley, Bishop, 52
Body of Christ, 139, 143, 144, 155, 156, 157, 187
Browne, Thomas, 46
Brunner, Emil, 56, 102, 178 ff.
Buber, Martin, 166
Bunyan, John, 86
Butterfield, H., 102

Calvin, John, 151, 177
Christ, 28, 56, 102 ff., 107, 110, 142, 178
  idea of, 103
  incognito, 103
  in the Trinity, 63–64
  redeemer, 31, 96, 133
  See atonement, Jesus
Church, the
  dual nature of, 136–137, 153, 155
  Early, 99, 169
  in history, 187
  in New Testament, 138 ff.
  on earth, 153 ff.
  uniqueness, 143
  See Body of Christ
churches, 16, 153 ff.
  See denominations
Clement, 140
Cohen, Morris, 161, 162
community, 87, 90
consubstantiation, 150
Copernicus, 14, 34
Creation stories, 76, 90
crucifixion, 101, 108–109, 123, 128
cultural change, 13–15, 28, 34, 36, 155

Darwin, Charles, 35
death, 81, 86–89, 117–120
decision, 16, 25, 29, 78, 85, 106–107, 179, 182–183
denominations, 138, 153, 156–157

depth psychology, 87
See also "we"
Descartes, René, 14, 52, 83–84
determinism, 78, 82–83
Docetism, 109
"double decree," 176, 178 ff.
doubt, 16
dread. *See Angst*
duty, 54, 77–79

ecumenical, 138, 144, 150, 168
Edison, Thomas, 60–61
end (of history), 128, 171 ff.
eschatology, 169, 171–172, 183–184
ethics, 54, 67, 126–129, 146, 174–175
evil, 31, 70, 107 ff., 120 ff., 125
evolution, 37, 61

faith, 14, 15–17, 20–23, 24–25, 42–43, 56, 57
"faith situation," 22, 24, 30
fear, 80 ff., 93
Final (Last) Judgment, 174 ff., 181
forgiveness, 27, 63, 134–135
Fosdick, Harry Emerson, 112
Frank, Eric, 56
freedom, 78, 82–83, 103, 120 ff., 177, 179
Freud, Sigmund, 18
fundamental contradiction, 95, 104
fundamentalists, 15, 36–38

Gethsemane, 106
Gnosticism, 109
"go beyond," 78 ff., 84
God
ambiguity, 60
as Father Almighty, 62, 65
as finite, 122
as Holy Spirit, 64–65
as person, 65
as process, 18–19
Creator, 27, 31, 50, 58, 61–62
Holy, 68–69
in Bible, 46 ff.
indescribable, 46–47, 56–57
in Jesus Christ, 63
in nature, 62–63
Joachim de Floris, 163–164
Judge, 67
Lord, 66
Love, 65
Mysterium Tremendum, 57, 69
no proof for, 49
responsibility of, 166
self-revelation of, 58–59, 60, 61, 63
unity of, 60
Wholly Other, 57, 58

Hilton, James, 164
historical, history, 62, 98, 160 ff., 186–187
Holy Spirit, 64–65, 138, 143
Hume, David, 56
Huxley, Aldous, 164
Huxley, Julian, 32

idealists, 17, 92
idols, 46–48
immortality, 117 ff.
incarnation, 103, 116, 124–126

Jesus, 73, 98 ff., 100, 102, 104, 107, 108
as Christ, 63, 97, 102 ff., 107, 116
resurrection of, 110 ff.
teachings of, 38, 72, 110, 139 ff., 168 ff.
See Christ
Johnson, Robert C., 100
judgment, 27, 79, 82
See Final Judgment

Kant, Immanuel, 53, 54, 56
Kierkegaard, Sören, 16–17, 80, 86, 93, 115
Kingdom of God, 31, 76, 142, 153, 159, 163, 165 ff., 174, 185–186
as coming gradually, 170
as coming suddenly, 169
as here now, 171, 183 ff.
knowledge, 60–61, 84
Koestler, Arthur, 23

Last (Lord's) Supper, 106, 143, 149–153
liberals, 15, 37, 41
Luther, Martin, 150, 151, 178

man, men
as animal, 76, 82
as creator, 82, 83, 87
as creature, 20, 77, 82–83
as image of God, 77
limitations of, 20, 58, 76
resistance of, 91 ff.
spiritual capacities of, 77 ff.
Maury, Pierre, 135
Messiah, 97, 167, 168
See Christ
Messianic Hope, 165–168
miracles, 40

naturalists, naturalism, 17 ff., 21, 24 ff., 29, 31, 61, 76, 77
nature, 18, 61–63, 76
Niebuhr, Reinhold, 72, 92, 187

Origen, 177
Orwell, George, 164
Otto, Rudolf, 57, 69
oughtness. *See* duty

Parousia, 139, 143
Pentecost, 143
Peter's confession, 140 ff.
Phillips, J. B., 150
philosophy
arguments for God, 49–58
limitations of, 47–49, 54–55, 57
of history, 159 ff.
process, 18–19
progress, 62, 161, 163–165, 170
Protestant, 34, 89, 137, 139, 150, 156
purgatory, 177

rational empirical method, 14, 48, 57, 160
redemption, 31, 134–135
religion, 27, 28, 58, 62, 75, 187
resurrection, 27, 31, 110 ff., 117, 120 ff., 127 ff., 174 ff.
retribution, doctrine of, 71 ff.
revelation, 14, 28, 57, 58, 125
revolution, intellectual, 13–14, 34 ff.
Richardson, Alan, 21
Roman Catholic, 89, 131, 139, 150, 156, 177

Rousseau, J. J., 159
Russell, Bertrand, 18

sacraments, 147 ff.
Sartre, J. P., 18, 161
scientific method, 30–31
Sermon on the Mount, 101, 107
sin, 67, 89 ff.
  as resistance, 93 ff.
  forgiveness for, 68, 134–135
  original, 89 ff.
Socrates, 16, 118
Spiegelberg, Herbert, 57
suicide, 79
supranaturalists, supranaturalism, 17–20, 24, 26–27, 29, 88, 126
sympathetic-antipathy, 93

temptations, the, 104 ff.
Tertullian, 21
Thomas, George, 134
Tillich, Paul, 54, 56, 69, 94, 97, 100, 118, 119, 161
Toynbee, Arnold J., 60, 162
Troeltsch, Ernst, 185
truth, 14, 15 ff., 29 ff., 38, 48–49

van de Velt, Th., 91

"we," 87–92
Wells, H. G., 109, 164
Westminster Confession, 34, 44
Whale, J. S., 52, 57
Wieman, Henry N., 19
Word of God, 34–36, 41, 46

Zoroastrianism, 62, 163
Zwingli, Ulrich, 151